LOVE IGNITES PEACE™
Our Next Evolution

By Paige Farrington

Published by Hearts of Humanity Publications, LLC Castle Rock, Colorado USA

ISBN: 979-8-9884473-2-0 (paperback edition)

*This book is dedicated to your
beautiful heart and your powerful mind.
May you find your way to unconditional love.*

Contents

Foreword

I first met Paige back in 2010, when we became friends through a mutual acquaintance. At one point after I met her, she and her daughter became my vocal students. I remember Paige practicing *Hey Jude*, singing it with the purest passion and joy. It may be one of the most delightful performances by one of my voice students that I ever experienced.

We remained connected as friends through the years, and I remember when she began speaking about how the idea of Love Ignites Peace entered her life. She spoke so bravely about how those three words landed in her mind, and I knew something special was transpiring for her. Words are powerful entities. However, I had no idea back then that those three simple words contained a deeper meaning that could powerfully change minds. I have been so lucky to have learned so much about love from Paige!

Love Ignites Peace continued to steep and grow within her, and then right at the end of 2018, she asked me to join her on her journey to begin writing about it. She was ready to begin growing her message to share it with the world, and she jumped into her work as a writer wholeheartedly. Over these last few years, she has honed herself into such a clear and expressive writer, and with her first book, *Love Ignites Peace: Our Next Evolution*, she now transforms herself into an author.

In this book you will encounter her life stories, and the stories of others surrounding her, all of which serve to illuminate the core experiences of our human existence. Paige digs deeply into her own journey, and I know that through her stories you will feel pieces of your own story being told. Her teachings regarding love, and its power to ignite peace for the planet, have the potential to change your mind, to change your perspectives on your past and future, and to remake you into a force for love in your own life and the lives of those around you. She teaches that love must start with you learning to love yourself, fully and deeply; and once you embody that love, it will unfurl out from you into the world.

I am fortunate and grateful to have traveled with Paige on her writing journey, from the early discussions about Love Ignites Peace, to seeing it printed on the pages of her very own book. Get ready! This book might just change your mind and incite your growth.

Happy reading!

—AnnaBeth H. Davidson
Editor

A Note from the Author

Through my personal stories, I hope you will find a safe refuge to explore the *information* contained within your stories. Following the breadcrumbs of your stories reveals the patterns that have challenged you in your relationships. When the message Love Ignites Peace charts your course, you empower love as your lifestyle and become a momentum builder for peace. The result—healthy and healed relationships, especially the one with yourself.

When the Universe unexpectedly gave me the words Love Ignites Peace, I was a million miles away from embodying the truth of those three words as my lifestyle. Venturing into deeper self-awareness felt daunting. Being honest about my deepest fears felt scary and unsafe. At that time, barely a flicker of self-love burned in my heart, but a flicker was all I needed; just enough, to encourage my journey towards greater self-awareness. Your self-love, whether you know it as a scarcely discernible spark or a roaring fire, is there to nurture your heart and to support you as you breakdown the narratives that have kept you from unconditionally loving yourself and others. Having the courage and vulnerability to reflect on your stories has an interesting effect. When you confront what has kept you feeling limited and small, those feelings begin to lose the power they once had over you.

Enjoy this book for its stories or return to it many times for deeper self-understanding. Every time you read this book the wisdom will become more illuminated in your everyday life. If the words inspire you to venture even further into your own process of self-discovery, consider writing about it using *Love Ignites Peace: Our Next Evolution, The Companion Journal*. This was written to help you unearth the behavior patterns and self-beliefs that keep you from unconditionally loving yourself and others.

As you assimilate the words within, you will raise your vibration and expand your consciousness (self-awareness). It is my greatest hope that you will feel loved, supported, and safe as you walk the parallel paths of unconditional self-love and love of others. Please know that I am holding space for you as you activate the love in your personal evolution, and deepen your relationship with yourself as you journey through your experiences.

You are the ONE—*Our Next Evolution*—that you and the world have been waiting for.

With Love,
Paige Farrington

Introduction

In 2008 the three words *Love Ignites Peace* were given to me. I wasn't asking for them, nor did I have any idea they were coming. Out of nowhere, like a lightning strike from a blue sky, the words *Love Ignites Peace* struck me unprepared and unaware. They burned themselves into my conscious mind. They arrived with no instruction manual or guidance as to their purpose; just three simple words impregnated with a powerful, yet simple message. So what was I to do with them? It has taken me 15 years to figure that out.

Most of those years were spent unraveling my own set of beliefs that were keeping me from unconditionally loving myself, so I could love others with compassion and understanding. I discovered that my most important relationship is the one with myself, because what I believe about myself affects the day-to-day life that I create. It determines how I interact with my family, my friends, my contentious relationships, and the entire human community. How I believe about myself determines my relationship with love.

From that moment through the present day, I've been on a journey to learn about and to embody the vast and uncontainable meanings of love, and to uncover the belief patterns that kept me from living love, as both a feeling and an action. It was from the darkness within me that my desire to learn how to live *Love Ignites Peace* grew deep and strong.

Love enabled me to face all of the things I was most afraid of, so I could start peeling back the layers of why I was afraid. Love showed me the path to understanding and forgiveness for myself and others, by showing me that we are all actors in a drama who create experiences for each other. Love forced me to take responsibility for all of my life experiences, especially those that kept me feeling victimized. Love required I make some huge life changes, like leaving my husband and creating a life that supported my love of self. Love taught me about the human experience. Sometimes love causes us to grow beyond the circumstances we have chosen.

Learning to live *Love Ignites Peace* is a journey for all of us, a tour-de-self that is well worth the effort. As I learned along the way, the only person I could change was me and the most important relationship I had was the one with myself. This adventure has not always been easy, but every bit of it has produced a happier, healthier, on-fire-with-life version of me.

The mental and emotional suffering from my old beliefs is gone and the joy from my new beliefs is fully installed. This was a process of healing my not-so-positive self-beliefs so that my heart could be wide open to loving without strings attached. It was an inner exploration that transformed my external relationships.

The love at *Love Ignites Peace* starts with self-love, expands outward to all of your relationships, and eventually becomes so filled with wisdom that you can offer compassion and acceptance to people you've never even met. We are all part of the same human community. *Love Ignites Peace* starts with you and eventually, when your self-love has grown strong and deep, with a higher vision and expanded self-awareness (consciousness), you can offer love as an action to your human community.

Think of love as a ladder, and on the bottom rung where you start your human journey is *love of self*. That self-love determines the ease or the challenges you will encounter as you climb love's ladder. If the rung of your self-love is weak and unstable, as you love others (like your family, friends, or romantic partners), the rungs won't hold the weight of your not-so-positive self-beliefs. This, in turn causes you mental and emotional suffering, and conflict within your relationships. You lash out because you are hurt. Conflict breeds more conflict and hurt creates more hurt. Learning to love yourself can feel a little like the game *Chutes and Ladders*.

As you feel love for others and then experience pain from those relationships, you slide back down the ladder. When you head back up, you create those same behavior patterns and experiences again, sometimes with different people and sometimes within the same relationships. This happens over and over until you realize and identify your not-love (more on not-love later) self-beliefs as creating the relationship patterns you replay over and over. *Love Ignites Peace* is a process of making that bottom rung strong with your love of self so you can, with confidence, offer love as an action to others. It is a personal evolution of breaking the patterns that create your negative feelings and behaviors—the ones that are out of alignment with your love of self. It is a tour-de-self that starts with you. As you change those internal patterns, you change how you interact with the external world.

As we align our self-beliefs with unconditional love (and yes I do believe unconditional love is possible for every human being), then the steps leading outward from our hearts can enable us to love others with understanding, discernment, allowing, forgiveness, acceptance, and respect. As you take that self-love up the ladder into your family life, you will feel more peaceful and be able to love even the more challenging family members. The same for friends. When you love yourself, you don't look to your romantic partner to fill the void of your not-love. You can then love them with all of your power because you aren't looking to them to make you feel loved.

With each higher step on the ladder, you move closer to offering love to your human community. That doesn't mean you have feelings for that stranger like you have for your family and friends, but it means you respect their unique life experiences. We are all on the same journey back to loving ourselves. As more and more people choose to live *Love Ignites Peace* individually, an unstoppable movement will take flight; a community of phoenixes arising from the rubble of our self-destruction. To change the collective consciousness, you must change your individual consciousness first.

Living Love Ignites Peace helps you build
a strong and lasting path to loving yourself,
while walking a parallel path to loving others.
Walking both paths is how you fully embody
the statement "Love Ignites Peace."

Imagine an old-fashioned fulcrum scale, with the bowls hanging from each side of the axis. Each individual's beliefs on this topic, though different, contain the same mass. Now imagine putting the beliefs that violence solves violence in one bowl, and the beliefs that there are other more peaceful ways to solve conflict in the other bowl. From what we see in the media and the decisions our leaders make, we've been programmed to believe that violence and self-righteousness resolves conflict, therefore the bowl with that consciousness tips to the table, while the other bowl sways near the top of the fulcrum's angled arm.

For the scales to become more in balance, individuals from the violence/self-righteousness side need to change their beliefs. What we've seen and experienced has made us believe that peace is impossible. This is another belief on the scales of balance that we need to change. As an individual changes their personal beliefs to *Love's 6 Actions* (read on to discover these powerful actions), they move to the other bowl. When enough of us change ourselves, the scales begin to balance and then they tip to the other direction.

If 51% of us acted and believed that peace was possible, and all beliefs contained the same mass, filtering the chaos of the world through *Love's 6 Actions,* the scales of balance would begin tipping to a new set of beliefs as the majority. Once the scales begin to tip, the possibility of a greater percentage of humanity changing their beliefs explodes exponentially. The law of critical mass as studied in both physics and sociology illustrates this phenomenon. The only way for the collective consciousness to change is for us to change our individual consciousness. *We change the collective consciousness by changing ourselves first.* Learning to become the words *Love Ignites Peace* changes *us,* changing the make-up of our collective human community.

Humans are not hardwired to hurt, control, struggle, suffer, and kill each other; we are hardwired for love. Humans are innately good. You are innately good. However, because of power's misuse, whether it is perpetuating fear, or the need for control, or all of our conditioning around lack, including lack of safety, our minds have been programmed with self-beliefs that keep us limited and hurting ourselves and each other. Conflict only creates more conflict and perpetuates more suffering for all of us. The thoughts and beliefs that make up our subconscious human operating system have erected a glass ceiling that has restricted our ability to evolve beyond these harmful behaviors.

Albert Einstein said that our problems cannot be solved from the same mindset that created them. Conflict, hate, fear, separation, violence, judgment, inequality, and self-righteousness, qualities that I call not-love, will not lead us to peace. Nor will they lead us to happiness, prosperity, and freedom. But love will. Living love as an action is the right use of our energy and that energy has the power to override the old ways of misusing power.

Love Ignites Peace is here to help you create new beliefs for yourself, and to change how we as a human community interact with each other. It takes both courage and vulnerability to look at your own behavior patterns and then choose who you want to become. New beliefs and behavior patterns have to replace old beliefs and patterns.

You are the *ignites* (the ignition) in *Love Ignites Peace.* Your inner fire of desire for a happy, peaceful, and abundant life opens your heart to becoming more self-aware. Do you love yourself enough to ignite your journey to peace, joy, and so much more? Does the fire for equality and freedom for our collective human community burn within you? Like a rocket blasting into orbit, your heart acts as the ignition, the powerful blast, that launches you into solving these old problems from a new consciousness (self-awareness).

It is time for you to make a choice. Do you want to continue to suffer the consequences of these old beliefs, or do you want to birth new beliefs that create a different experience for yourself and our collective human community? Are you ready to shatter the ceiling of your limiting beliefs and unhealthy behavior patterns?

Love Ignites Peace brings a new consciousness to solving these old problems. It transforms our not-love beliefs so that we can break through that restrictive glass ceiling. We are each on an individual journey of becoming more self-aware, so we can evolve beyond the patterns that have kept us from living love's all-things-good energies. When we change, the collective begins to change too. *Love Ignites Peace* empowers each and every one of us to learn how to fully love ourselves, so that we can love our human community.

> *It is up to us, as individuals, to write a new set*
> *of beliefs and behaviors for ourselves so we can*
> *write a new set of beliefs for our collective human*
> *community, one person at a time. We cannot*
> *experience peace as a collective until we*
> *experience peace within ourselves.*

Love Ignites Peace is your personal and individual journey back to knowing, accepting, and loving yourself, first and foremost. As you truly love yourself then you can love others unconditionally. It is love of yourself and your ability to offer understanding, forgiveness, discernment, acceptance, allowing, and respect to all life that will create peace for our human community. Peace on earth, and the many other all-things-good energies that love generates, starts with you. You are the ignition, the fire that will create the change. Love as an action is the energy that creates your individual and then the collective transformation.

DEFINITIONS

Love Ignites Peace
A parallel journey of learning to love yourself while you are learning how to offer love as an action to others.

Consciousness
The state of being self-aware. This includes your perceptions of what is happening around you and to you. Your perceptions contribute to your self-beliefs and those beliefs create your self-awareness. Your self-awareness determines how you interact with love of self and love of others.

The Human Community's Collective Consciousness
The sum total of all individual consciousnesses, which equal the collective, unified, consciousness of humanity. When 51% of humanity's individual consciousness changes, the scales of balance tip and the unified collective consciousness changes.

1
The Birth of *Love Ignites Peace*

My journey to understanding and living *Love Ignites Peace* began several years before those three words ever entered my mind. Around age 33, after the birth of my second child, a strange thing began to happen in my mouth. Every time I would floss my teeth, my gums would bleed profusely, rivers of blood flowing from around each tooth. Yes, I went to the dentist. Yes, I took care of my teeth. This was a phenomenon well beyond periodontal disease. With each year the bleeding got worse. My dentist sent me to specialists. I was scheduled for surgery two different times to cut away gum tissue, but each time I canceled a few days before. Through the lens of their training and what they knew, the only explanation in the experts' minds was periodontal disease, a disease caused by not taking care of your teeth.

Because no dentist could diagnose my unusual predicament, my bleeding gums took me on a many years quest, trying to find out what on earth was causing the bleeding. The only path I knew at that time was allopathic, Western medicine. Each doctor would look at me like an alien walking off of a spaceship. They would ask, "Do you brush and floss your teeth?" "Yes," I would answer, "multiple times a day." Bloodwork was run. Nothing. This went on and on.

One winter day, I was again in the periodontist office for another deep cleaning, a four-hour and under-anesthetic process, feeling bereft and near hopeless that this mystery would ever be solved. In one of those meant-to-be moments in time, synchronicity in action, another patient jogged something in Dr. Shimoto's mind about a local female doctor whose approach was less conventional. Dr. Shimoto, with shoulders back and a bit of a swagger, walked into my treatment room and said, "I have someone for you to see who takes a more holistic approach. The patient in the other room speaks very highly of her diagnostic abilities."

Numb from the anesthetic and the perpetual unknowing of what was causing my health problems, I made an appointment. At my very first visit with her, she listened to me recite the diatribe of my very unusual symptoms. I mean, how many people show up at a doctor's office for profusely bleeding gums? Within the first 10 minutes she suggested I get tested for gluten intolerance. Two weeks later I began the process of eliminating gluten from my life. A few weeks after that, the bleeding stopped. I refer to this moment as the moment I got my life back. I was 39 years old.

What had gone unnoticed by me, as my health continued to slowly deteriorate, were all of the other things happening in my body. Each day, exhaustion overwhelmed me to the point that I had to rest in order to survive. An afternoon nap usually propped me up enough to get through the rest of the day. But if that didn't happen, by dinner time it took a herculean effort to feed my family, clean up the kitchen, and get everyone to bed. My 65-year-old mom could run circles around me. You might be asking, how could this level of continual, unceasing exhaustion go unnoticed? Though I managed as a functioning mother, wife, and business-woman, my mind felt like mud, the clarity of my thoughts filled with sediment. I had become unconscious and anesthetized to my life, and completely oblivious to the obvious.

Consuming gluten had taken me on a physical and mental journey into depletion and darkness. It had created inner static that disrupted my ability to hear myself, see myself, and feel myself. Once the static was gone, the message came through loud and clear: "Where have you gone?" Mentally and emotionally, I could hear, see, and feel myself again. My parents raised me in a loving household, filled with joy and laughter. At age 39, my feelings about life and myself barely resembled that spirited, life-loving girl.

It was subtle at first, but I started feeling glimpses of myself again. I had a bit more energy. The sky looked bluer and the grass greener, my senses reengaging. As the mental sludge dissipated, I began asking myself, "Who am I?" "Why had I made the decisions, I'd made?" "Where was the spir-ited, cheerleading, cartwheeling girl from my childhood?" My innate nature sparked with feistiness, but the spirited and bubbly Paige had been gone for years. Life used to spill over with joyfulness. Now everything felt like the color gray, the complexion of a sunless day. In the past, my inner fire ignited me to stand up for myself. But that Paige, that part of me, had gone missing, beaten down by the power of derogatory words and exhaustion, my sense of self impaled with belittling beliefs. My inner dialogue overflowed with viral self-judgment, self-punishment, self-dismissal, and unhappiness.

With tenacity, I began to seek all of the causes for my physical suffering. I soon discovered that there was more to me than just my physical body. There was the mental me which housed my perceptions and self-beliefs. There was the emotional me which stored the pain of my traumas. And there was the spiritual me, my divine self, which was calling me to release suffering and seek self-acceptance and self-love.

My mind now clear, I started each day with what I called quiet time. I'd sit in my yellow wing-backed chair, close my eyes and just breathe for 5 to 10 minutes, and then I'd read inspirational and thought-provoking material. Sometimes pen to paper, I'd journal about the old Paige and the current Paige. The energetic divergence between the two versions of me broke my heart with longing for the joy I used to feel about myself and life, along with the sad recognition for who I had become. Unbeknownst to me, my heart was guiding me, igniting my desire for *change within myself.* I knew I needed to end my marriage, but fortunately, at that time I was unable to take that step. Why fortunate? Because my husband and our relationship were my greatest teacher. Our unhealthy relationship, combined with my own fears, kept me asking myself "How did I end up feeling this unhappy?" Relentless questioning took me to the top of the cliff, and from there I dove headfirst into the deep waters of self-exploration.

I was terrified to leave my relationship, afraid to be responsible for my own life. Fear and self-distrust vibrated with such force that my heart pounded and my head buzzed with crisis-like adrenaline. When conversing with my husband my voice froze, a colossal iceberg, blocking my ability to say what I really wanted to say. The more he sensed me not speaking my truth, the angrier he acted towards me. Thawing this iceberg of fear and self-distrust became my unwavering focus. I was living a life so filled up with disempowerment, unhealthy boundaries, and taking responsibility for everyone's feelings, that who I truly was got lost/ buried.

There was a grand canyon between who I wanted to be and how I wanted to feel, and how I actually felt. I started with unpacking my suitcase of limiting self-beliefs. What were the beliefs that were causing me to feel not only unhappy, but so disempowered? I loved myself enough to want to feel happy again. I didn't want to settle for feeling afraid and unhappy.

Love Ignites Peace

Love melted my fears and taught me how to
stand authentically in my wholeness.

With relentless tenacity, I worked to uncover the self-beliefs and behavior patterns that governed how I acted and interacted with life, and the whys of my fear and self-distrust. As I unraveled the threads of my unhealthy and disempowered self-beliefs, I began to discover why I'd made certain choices and was incapable of speaking my truth. These prison-like programs fueled the not-love messages from my subconscious self-beliefs, my Machiavellian master, with the energies that kept me disconnected from unconditionally loving myself. All of these limiting self-beliefs were the opposite of love, they were not-love. Through this passionate journey of self-discovery, I came to understand how to live *Love Ignites Peace.*

Regaining my health served as the starting point for my journey to self-awareness and health, but an unknown force had bigger plans that expanded me well beyond my physical body. Two years after my gluten intolerance diagnosis, on a summer Colorado day that saturated every cell of my body with its perfection and beauty, the Universe delivered three words to me: *Love Ignites Peace.* The blue Colorado sky stretched like water above me, birds danced from tree to tree, serenading me as my mind relaxed into the story that was revealing itself through the pages of my novel. In front of me the lake reflected the trees and mountains on its watery canvas. I remember looking up from my book and breathing in the beauty, audibly sighing with gratitude and contentment.

As my head lowered to my book, the three words *Love Ignites Peace* landed solidly and without fanfare on the doorstep of my conscious mind. Eyes wide with surprise, my head jerked up and I said, "What???" *Love Ignites Peace*. My ears did not hear those words, but my mind saw them. Like hot coals to tender flesh, they were burned in my consciousness. Three commonplace words, yet unforgettable in their arrival. No instructions. No explanation. Just those three words. In that brief moment, *Love Ignites Peace* planted itself in my mind like seeds in a garden. Those seeds began to grow, no care instructions, no directions; just a deep inner desire to understand them and why they were given to me.

An unexplainable second of life's magic turned an ordinary moment in time into an unforgettable moment that left me astonished and wanting to know more. I abandoned my book and went for a walk, the physical movement of my body helping me process that moment and those three words. As I walked, another image arrived with lightning quickness and vivid clarity. I saw a heart, an arrow, a campfire, an arrow, and a peace sign. It reminded me of the childhood game where the message was decoded from the pictures.

These three words baffled me. I wrote them down. I drew them like I'd been shown. I stared at them. I meditated on them. They made perfect sense when intellectually read as Love -> Ignites-> Peace. They were a statement that contained a general truth; however, I had no idea what they actually meant or what I was suppose to do with them. I asked the forces of Higher Consciousness, "Help me to know why you gave me those three words. What do I do with them?"

Love Ignites Peace, a newborn in my consciousness required parenting. But, just like being a parent to an actual child, there was no instruction manual for how to raise my unique child. As parents, we all do the best we can through the filters of our own consciousness (self-awareness), sighing with relief when our children are raised and successfully on their own. *Love Ignites Peace* parented *me* with infinite patience to be a better me. My subconscious self-beliefs unceasingly interfered with my ability to live within love consciousness. *Love Ignites Peace* lived with me every day, pushing me to unravel what was keeping me from living that more understanding, less judgmental, and more forgiving and accepting version of myself.

Moments occurred, and sometimes they still do, when a person or situation sucks me back to feeling self-righteous, powerless, or not-enough, and it's within those reminders *Love Ignites Peace* challenges me to look deep inside. What in that interaction sparked my reaction? Then and now, *Love Ignites Peace* reminds me that *it* runs my life, not the not-love self-beliefs that cause me to feel self-judgment. The lines blur. Who is parenting whom? I parented the desire to live *Love Ignites Peace* within my life, but at the same time *Love Ignites Peace* parented me. The truth in the statement *Love*

Ignites Peace guides me back to who I really *am* and who I choose to *be*, the wisdom of love.

These two extraordinary moments in my life—when my mind cleared and my health improved, and when the three unexpected words *Love Ignites Peace* were delivered to my consciousness—galvanized me to nurture my self-love and magnificence into absoluteness. Over the next decade I progressed and then regressed while learning to embody the wisdom and understanding of unconditional self-love and unconditional love for others. It took me years to firmly stand in the power and oneness of love's accepting arms.

Love Ignites Peace is a journey; a personal growth trip unique to all of us, because we are all unique in how we perceive ourselves, our lives, and our human community. There is no one in the world exactly like you. Your DNA and the self-beliefs you've created from your life experiences differentiate you from everyone else on this planet. Exploring *Love Ignites Peace* caused me to deeply investigate myself. Along the way I learned about the human experience, which once I understood the complexities, plays like a game. Discovering the challenges, the rules, and the objective were all insights that enabled me to live *Love Ignites Peace's* powerful 3-word message. There is no one-size-fits-all on this unique journey back to self-love and love of others, though the challenges and the rules of the game are the same for all of us.

The first few years after receiving those three words, I kept asking "What am I to *do* with this?" When I was finally ready for the answer, the message came through loud and clear, "Learn how to live *Love Ignites Peace* in your own life." The question I then asked was, "How the heck do I live *Love Ignites Peace* in my life? Please show me The Way." I asked and I received. I learned about the human experience and duality's challenges, and I learned how to love myself and others using *Love's 6 Actions*. *Love Ignites Peace* beckoned me to look at my past, present, and future. It will beckon you to look at yours.

When you express your heart's desire to
become Love Ignites Peace, you open yourself
to receive the wisdom to make that happen.
Miracles will occur. Synchronicities, events that
seem to be related, but there is no correlation
which indicates that one is caused by the other, will
surprise you and move you closer to your desire.

Once my mind cleared, I began to feel deep within that I had a purpose, something that was well beyond my day-to-day work. So I asked, "I feel that I have a greater purpose, show me what that purpose is." I also strongly desired to return to the innately joyful person that once bubbled from within. Again I asked, "Show me what I need to do to find myself. Who I truly am." A miracle happened and like an unexpected meteor crashing in my conscious mind, the three words *Love Ignites Peace* arrived. At the time, I did not recognize the miracle or the magic, but now magic is all I see. Ask and you will receive.

The magic required for destination *Love Ignites Peace* comes entirely from within you. You are the ignition of your personal evolution, the magic of your everyday life. You are the force within yourself that inspires your desire to become love's consciousness.

> *Love elevates your feelings and your actions*
> *by knowing and recognizing you for who you*
> *truly are, so you can offer that same non-*
> *judgmental understanding, forgiveness,*
> *acceptance, and respect to others.*

Love Ignites Peace is the inner guidance system that routes and reroutes you back to loving yourself and others. It's the greatest gift you can give yourself and our collective human community.

HELPFUL HINT:

As you read my story and the other stories contained within these chapters, ask yourself, "Do I see myself reflected in any part of that story?" If the answer is yes, make a note so you can come back to that story later. As you read each chapter you will begin to understand the deep meanings contained in your own life's experiences. What are you reading that reflects a piece of you back to you?

Your challenge is to deeply understand yourself through the stories and the wisdom found in these pages.

2
Love vs. Not-Love

QUESTION FOR CONTEMPLATION
AS YOU DIGEST CHAPTER 2:

What stories and questions in this chapter
reflect back to you a quality or an experience
that you can identify with?

Long ago, I bought a tee-shirt that said, "Love is not something that you look for…love is something you become." Love is a becoming, a far-reaching tour-de-self that influences the way we interact with ourselves and each other. Love transformed me from unhappy, unhealthy, and disempowered to a peaceful person who loves life. For too long I looked outside of myself for love, hoping that someone else's love would make me feel whole and happy. That never happened. Love was my becoming, not my seeking.

Since I didn't fully love myself and my husband didn't fully love himself either, our relationship was fraught with challenges. His love lacked the ingredients to cause me to love myself and my love was never good enough to cause him to love himself. When we first got married, I believed my love was large enough for both of us, that I could fix those parts that he didn't love about himself. At the time I was unconscious to the parts in me that needed love too. As seekers of love, we looked to each other to fill our gaping wounds. I finally realized that my love couldn't change him, it could only change me. Instead of seeking love, I decided to become love, thanks to the message *Love Ignites Peace*. Love is a *starts with me* sort of becoming, because transformation is a very personal process. Only I understood myself well enough to know what I needed to repair.

Love is the most powerful four-letter word in our dictionary, because the actions connected with love create joy and harmony in our minds and hearts. Love as a verb (action) builds all things good and love as a noun is the builder of life's sweetness. We mostly think of love as a feeling. And it is a feeling that engineers happiness, joy, creativity, fulfillment, satisfaction, and contentment. We feel love for our family and our partners. We even feel love for some of our friends. But love is so much more than a feeling; it is a lifestyle filled with everyday actions, big and small, that create better lives and more health and happiness for everyone.

Why love? Because love turns your heart green with spring and your mind golden with sunshine. It warms you, comforts you, and lights you up with joy. Love is the nectar that sweetens your life. Love says to you, "I know your potential and I believe in you." Love transforms the limitations of fear and doubt into trust and confidence. Love blossoms into the freedom of acceptance. Love grows discernment. It seeks understanding and sheds the burdens of holding onto the past. Love allows us to learn from our experiences free of judgment. Love is the seed that grows the life that our individual hearts and our collective hearts most desire. Love doesn't need to be pruned or weeded, because it grows goodness. Goodness for all. Love connects you with the energies that fortify life. Love is the new consciousness, the answer, because love supports your highest good and the highest good of our collective human community.

Every human being on this planet wants to be loved and to love. Love is innately who we are. When our lifetime of accumulated self-beliefs is out of alignment with love, we experience emotional pain and suffering. We feel anger's disempowerment, judgment's lack, sadness's hurt, anxiety's fears, and depression's darkness. These emotions and their associated beliefs keep us spiraling in the vacuum of our old feelings and behavior patterns. They disempower us from saying what we want to say, taking action toward our dreams, and accepting ourselves just as we are. The mental and emotional discomfort generated from our fragmented self-love unknowingly produces a force inside of us that traps us underneath a glass ceiling, which holds us back from what we truly want to do, who we want to be, and how we genuinely want to feel.

What has caused all of this suffering? Words and actions

laced with judgment, control, fear, manipulation, degradation, not-enoughness, punishment, acrimony, self-righteousness, greed, and lack. These words, actions, and their associated feelings, speak a language that programs our mental/emotional pain and suffering. I call these actions and any other actions that do not support a person's potential, not-love. Not-love is the harmful opposite of love. Not-love has never solved any problem, it only creates hurt and suggests to a person that they aren't 100% lovable. Not-love is the past, and love is our future.

Why love? Because love announces that your wants, your needs, your dreams, and your feelings matter; that you matter. Love empowers your dreams into reality, your hurt into healing, and your limitations into your potential. From dreams as simple as *I want to feel happy*, to as grandiose as *I want to sail around the world in my multi-million dollar yacht*, self-love empowers you to shatter your glass ceiling of limitations and to create the life that you most desire by embodying your authentic self.

Your authentic self is the part of you that gives you permission to explore what interests you and to express it in alignment with what makes you feel good about yourself. Love encourages you to listen to the deepest parts of yourself, because love wants you to be exactly who you want to be, to fully enjoy your life and life's multitude of experiences, and to create new experiences that feed your joy. Love is the action, the new language, that has the power to heal the inner chaos, the conflict, and the limitations that not-love has inflicted.

We speak words and act in ways that cause separation and suffering because our experiences can lead us to believe that is how we should act. We live on a planet where everything has an opposite; this is known as duality. We've operated from the negative or fear-based side of duality and those not-love words and actions have programmed our minds to believe that there is something wrong with us. Our beliefs fuel our feelings and our actions. When we believe we aren't enough, we treat ourselves and others as such.

Not-enoughness was one of my personal epidemics that kept me spiraling with beliefs that I wasn't smart enough, kind enough, cute enough, and my body certainly wasn't enough to make me loveable. When we change our beliefs, we change how we think about ourselves. I couldn't love myself if I didn't believe I was enough for myself or good enough for a romantic partner to love me. What we believe influences our behavior, directly determining how we treat ourselves and others.

Comparing our beliefs to the operating system of a computer demonstrates how our beliefs generate the output of our behaviors. A computer is coded with a programming language that makes the computer operate (behave) in a certain way. The operating system contains all of the code/instructions that generate the output of its applications. Our belief systems are our personal human operating system.

As we observe what is going on outside of us (our environment), we create meanings about ourselves that become our self-beliefs. Those self-beliefs get stored in our sub, or below conscious awareness mind. Our subconscious mind, filled with thousands of self-beliefs, both good and not so good, becomes our human operating system. Those beliefs then produce the output of our thoughts, feelings, and behaviors. If our beliefs are aligned with disempowerment and drama, then that is how we will behave. If our beliefs are aligned with understanding and acceptance, then that is how we will treat ourselves and others.

Our minds are like sponges that absorb every word, every gesture, every action, every smell, every sound, every taste, along with the non-verbal reactions and feelings of others. These sponge-like capabilities are heightened from in-utero until age 7, when most of our self-beliefs are installed. But the subconscious mind's belief systems can be re-programmed at any time. I experienced this myself within my marriage, as my self-worth decomposed, little by little, because of the damaging words we exchanged.

Not believing I was worthy disconnected me from my happiness and my health. The belief, *unworthy*, secretly wrote lines of contaminated code in my operating system that disempowered my ability to love and accept myself. As humans we have trouble seeing beyond our beliefs. These beliefs, constructed through words and actions, have built our relationship with ourselves and others. If we want change, then we have to start cleaning out our closet of beliefs and decide what we want to keep and what to throw away.

Why love? Because love challenges us to become more self-aware and to look at our own beliefs. When we are ready, love empowers us to *become* the change we desire. Love is the free energy source that can transform the past and supply the future with unlimited goodness, helping us understand what keeps us from loving ourselves.

You weren't taught to discern love from not-love as you negotiated the many roads of your relationships. You accepted what people said to you, about you, and you unknowingly created meanings about who you thought you were from those interactions. How people treated you indirectly taught you about love as an action. People loved and encouraged you, they hurt you, they modeled love and not-love behaviors, and your mind, unbeknownst to you, told you how you should believe about yourself and how you should act based on how others were treating you and how they were behaving.

As you observed people interacting with others, you created self-perceptions about how other people interacted with love or not-love. If you didn't have the self-awareness to run each experience through a filter that was able to separate loving words and actions from not-love words and actions, then you adopted some loving and some not-loving actions as part of your self-beliefs.

How did your influential role models treat the people

they loved and those that they didn't? Were they kind or were they mean? How did they solve problems? Did they blame and shame or take personal responsibility for their actions? Did they seek attention by manipulating? Were they controlling or accepting? Did they support your interests or make you feel guilt or fear for pursing what you wanted to explore?

As you observed and personally experienced the behaviors of your parents and others, you created meanings about yourself, and those meanings became your self-beliefs. You unknowingly taught yourself about love or not-love from your relationships. Those beliefs then determined your behavior.

I was fortunate to be raised in a home where we treated each other with love and kindness. My parents' behaviors toward others and their words and actions toward me reflected those energies, thus I was "programmed" with self-beliefs that told me that treating others with love and kindness was how I should behave.

My close friend Hannah was born into a family where the children were treated as inconveniences. She and her sisters were told by their father never to have children, because children were an unnecessary nuisance. When her father was angry he would get into her face and overpower her to make his point. Thus, Hannah adopted self-beliefs that told her she was not wanted and that the best way to solve problems was to bully another person with her scalpel-sharp words. The love (not-love) she saw modeled equaled rejection and conflict to her self-beliefs.

Most of us know that being kind and compassionate creates positive and loving results. However, the self-beliefs that we learned from observing others don't always align with kindness, respect, empathy, and compassion. It is from your not-love self-beliefs that you become triggered by other people's words and actions. Those same self-beliefs cause you to hurt and limit yourself and others also. There is nothing loving about living from lack and unhappiness or manipulation and self-righteousness.

Not-love's self-talk keeps your mind spiraling on thoughts that keep you small and afraid. Not-love promotes suffering. What happens when we feel the pain of not-love? We end up hurting others with our words and actions. Just like love is an action, so too is not-love, and we have a long history of interacting with not-love.

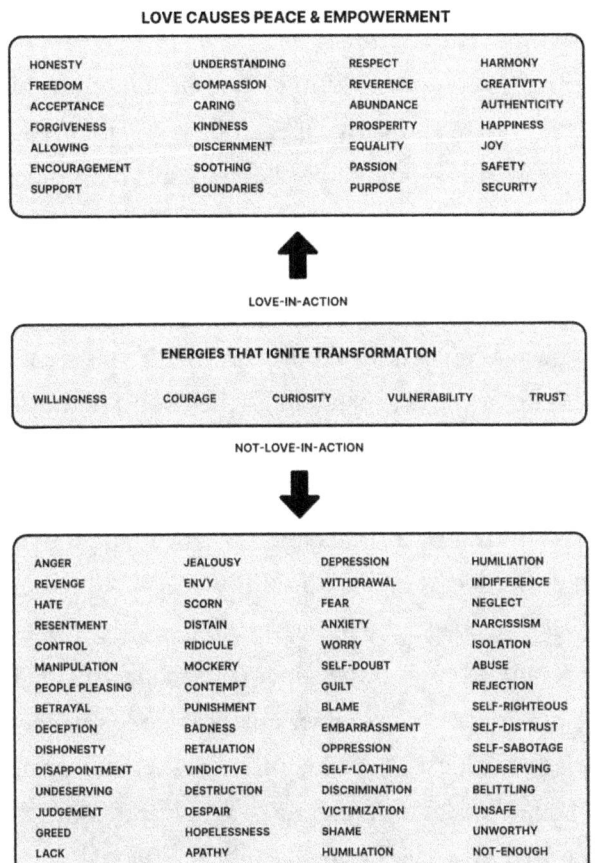

LOVE CAUSES PEACE & EMPOWERMENT

HONESTY	UNDERSTANDING	RESPECT	HARMONY
FREEDOM	COMPASSION	REVERENCE	CREATIVITY
ACCEPTANCE	CARING	ABUNDANCE	AUTHENTICITY
FORGIVENESS	KINDNESS	PROSPERITY	HAPPINESS
ALLOWING	DISCERNMENT	EQUALITY	JOY
ENCOURAGEMENT	SOOTHING	PASSION	SAFETY
SUPPORT	BOUNDARIES	PURPOSE	SECURITY

LOVE-IN-ACTION

ENERGIES THAT IGNITE TRANSFORMATION

WILLINGNESS	COURAGE	CURIOSITY	VULNERABILITY	TRUST

NOT-LOVE-IN-ACTION

ANGER	JEALOUSY	DEPRESSION	HUMILIATION
REVENGE	ENVY	WITHDRAWAL	INDIFFERENCE
HATE	SCORN	FEAR	NEGLECT
RESENTMENT	DISTAIN	ANXIETY	NARCISSISM
CONTROL	RIDICULE	WORRY	ISOLATION
MANIPULATION	MOCKERY	SELF-DOUBT	ABUSE
PEOPLE PLEASING	CONTEMPT	GUILT	REJECTION
BETRAYAL	PUNISHMENT	BLAME	SELF-RIGHTEOUS
DECEPTION	BADNESS	EMBARRASSMENT	SELF-DISTRUST
DISHONESTY	RETALIATION	OPPRESSION	SELF-SABOTAGE
DISAPPOINTMENT	VINDICTIVE	SELF-LOATHING	UNDESERVING
UNDESERVING	DESTRUCTION	DISCRIMINATION	BELITTLING
JUDGEMENT	DESPAIR	VICTIMIZATION	UNSAFE
GREED	HOPELESSNESS	SHAME	UNWORTHY
LACK	APATHY	HUMILIATION	NOT-ENOUGH

NOT-LOVE CAUSES SUFFERING & DISEMPOWERMENT

Not love also shows up in your life as other people's expectations of you. Not all expectations are harmful, but many are. Expectations put pressure on you and those pressures don't always align with what you desire. Expectations come from many sources: from your parents, partners, friends, teachers, and your religious training. All of the expectations that feel uncomfortable to you should be explored, because it's possible those expectations aren't who you truly are or want to be. The media and culture should be added to that list, as they inundate you with expectations that show you what they believe you should look like; making the standard for what is good and therefore "loveable" unachievable for most of us.

What has the messaging from these various sources done to what you believe about yourself? If you are judging yourself about these expectations, then you are most likely judging others too. These not-love expectations that are fed into you cause you to feed those same expectations into others, thus continuing a cycle of not-love in action for you and for our collective human community.

I was a teenager in the early 1980's when the fashion industry started promoting super thin models as the norm. Eating disorders became a serious problem as women and men tried to achieve waif-like thinness. I remember not eating so I could make my bones more visible under my clothes, because that is what the media told me looked good. The meaning I created from that belief, without self-awareness, was that if I was super skinny then I would be more lovable. Big breasts for women then became a style, along with maintaining thinness. And now everyone wants a plump rear end.

Who creates these trends and what do these trends do to your ability to fully and completely love yourself? I spent years disentangling and then overcoming the list of self-beliefs that told me my body wasn't good enough, along with other physical "imperfections" that kept me from believing I was enough.

These expectations hurt you and make it difficult to fully love and accept yourself, just as you are. They create mental and emotional suffering, and sometimes even physical suffering when you don't meet the expectations. A gay friend, who was raised with strict religious beliefs, believed that because he was gay God didn't love him. These expectations sometimes were so heavy that they extinguished his happiness and caused him anxiety.

Another friend was raised by parents who expected him to be perfect in everything he did. From school to sports, he was expected to be the best. He became a workaholic who was always reaching for unattainable perfection. He disregarded others to fulfill his achievements. Alone and filled with anxiety, he finally realized that the expectations put on him at an early age had corrupted his self-beliefs and caused him to hurt others and himself, so that he could be enough for his parents.

When you plug in *Love Ignites Peace* as the destination into your mental GPS, it empowers you to become more self-aware. What is causing you to feel unhappy with yourself, or anxious, or uncomfortable in your own skin? What is preventing you from unconditionally loving and accepting yourself? What is keeping you disempowered and unable to take action toward what makes you happy?

When you can love yourself, your mental and emotional suffering goes away because there aren't any self-beliefs keeping you limited and telling you that you aren't loveable. There is no hurt left inside of you that causes you to hurt yourself and others. If you aren't judging yourself, then you have no need to judge others. The language of love as an action begins with you. Your self-love empowers others to love themselves too.

Your most important relationship is the one with yourself, because that relationship determines how you behave in your other relationships. If you unconditionally love and accept yourself then you can easily offer that same love to others, even strangers. Becoming more self-aware about the beliefs keeping you from self-love is an ongoing process that strengthens your relationship with yourself. While you are discovering how to love yourself, you can also start to offer that same love and acceptance to others. Love as an action spreads in a very non-linear way because love is an all-inclusive process. Self-awareness is required to dissect what prevents you from loving yourself and your inability to offer love as an action to others.

Love as an action is a language you must learn to speak. How were you raised? What were you taught about love? What did love add up to for you? Kindness? Conflict? Compassion? Manipulation? Generosity? Disappointment? Anger? Understanding? Self-righteousness? Acceptance? Control? Respect? Encouragement? Guilt? It may not be just one of these, it may be several or all of them, or concepts I didn't mention. Take a minute and connect with your self-awareness. What are the self-beliefs that you hold around love as an action? You can't change what you aren't aware of.

If your relationships exemplified not-love to your young mind, it is possible that some of those not-love behaviors unknowingly became the self-beliefs you associated with love and with safety. Others' not-love actions toward you instigated the not-love self-beliefs that you unknowingly created about yourself. Your ego, your great inner illusionist, secretly whispered to your psyche that those not-love self-beliefs would keep you safe and protect you from more not-love, even though those beliefs were in conflict with your happiness and your potential.

When you were shamed or made to feel guilty for wanting what you desired, or manipulated, yelled at, told you were a disappointment, made to feel undeserving, blamed, bullied, ridiculed, or shunned, your ego, from the subconscious meanings you created about yourself, twisted your mental suffering into unseeable prisons of perceived safety. Though you might have hungered for a different outcome, those not-love words and actions imprinted themselves in your mind and through the patterns of familiarity. They deceptively made you believe that they were keeping you safe. There is no safety in not-love, only suffering and limitation.

The devious parts of my ego told me that if I spoke honestly about what I was really feeling people wouldn't like/

love me. What if my honesty hurt the other person, even if they were hurting me? Of course I didn't deserve friends; yes, it was always my fault. I was a disappointment because I didn't meet society's expectations.

From these experiences and others, I installed the belief that I had to prove myself in everything I did and who I was. I had to prove that I was likable, loveable, and smart. These not-love self-beliefs became the "safety" mechanisms that patterned my behavior in my relationships. I created situations where I felt like I was a disappointment, and then I had to make amends and prove that I wasn't. I attracted people into my life that affirmed that I didn't deserve friends.

My people-pleasing ways overcompensated by encouraging me to build up the people who preyed on my need to please them. I also found safety in disconnecting emotionally. I couldn't be hurt by what I couldn't feel. It just wasn't safe for me to unconditionally love myself or to love others because of the not-love self-beliefs that I'd stashed in my subconscious human operating system.

The irony of how our ego tricks us is that we continue to create suffering for ourselves as we pattern our behaviors from the not-love that influenced the meanings we unknowingly created about ourselves. Those not-love beliefs stored in our subconscious human operating systems become our ego's ammunition. My dishonesty, because I felt too afraid to speak my truth, only created more hurt and harsh words from those that could sense my disempowerment.

True change in your consciousness begins when you start to understand that as humans we are not only seeking love, but safety and security too. Becoming self-aware is how you discern when not-love in action is what is keeping you seemingly *safe,* but you are actually spiraling in behavior patterns that create suffering. Self-awareness empowers you to explore all of the ways that other people's behaviors toward you have made you feel unsafe and unprotected.

When you don't feel safe, the people that are supposed to love and protect you unknowingly fill your mind with insecurities and feelings that you aren't worthy/ enough/deserving of being yourself. My friend Jude was raised by an angry father who he could never seem to please. His household walked on eggshells because they never knew what would set the Colonel off, from a toy that was left out to missing a tackle on the football field.

Jude lived with uncertainty of what his actions might do to set his dad into a tirade that resulted in a verbal and often physical punishment. Through that lack of feeling safe, Jude's subconscious self-beliefs fueled by his ego's need for safety, started to tell little lies. His lies were used to protect himself and to redirect blame. It just wasn't safe for him to be responsible for his own actions, because the consequences of being himself were too great.

Another friend, who was sexually assaulted by a friend of her family, was left to deal with the fallout of her feelings, because her mom and the rest of her family never protected her before or after the assault. This created a depressive spiral fed by self-beliefs that told her she didn't matter and wasn't important enough to be protected by her mom.

Lack of safety, another harmful expression of not-love, vandalizes our psyche; then, in a duplicitous twist of deceit, it makes us believe our not-love self-beliefs are keeping us safe. We might think being dishonest, needing to people-please or over-inflating our greatness are actions that are protecting us.

The cacophony of voices that lobbed or even catapulted not-love words at you were operating from a consciousness (self-awareness or lack thereof) that told them their not-love actions were keeping them safe too. For some, the only way they knew how to convey love was from the not-love they had learned and then unknowingly adopted as their self-beliefs.

Think about a mother who is filled with insecurities. As a child you don't know that your mom is unsettled, but you receive love from a mom who then uses guilt and manipulation to keep your love for her close. Imagine a father who enforces his rigid belief system, the very system that is keeping him safe, onto his children. A young mind has no idea that his father is filled with fear of what might happen if he allows himself or others to explore beyond the stiff box he built to contain himself. The love received from this father stifles, creates fear, and limits exploration. A bully doesn't make fun of people because they feel good about themselves, a bully causes pain because they are in pain.

Not-enoughness invaded my subconscious human operating system with a mental virus that caused me to suffer in my romantic relationships. As a result, I was attracted to the men that thought I wasn't enough, and I rejected the ones that treated me like I was. Not-being enough kept me believing that I was safe only when I was with men who were treating me like I wasn't enough. Not being enough also showed up in my need to constantly prove myself. Not-love has created a tidal wave of disempowering self-beliefs and unhappy feelings that have kept us recreating and reinstalling those same patterns over and over in the people we love and other relationships. We have created not-love in our collective human community, one person at a time, with how we have interacted with each other.

Living *Love Ignites Peace* is an individualized journey of becoming more self-aware so you can transform your self-beliefs (the unhealthy, not-love patterns) that you acquired from your life's experiences into behaviors that align with love as an action. When you do this you are not only transforming the relationship with yourself, but also how others come to believe about themselves.

ENERGIES THAT IGNITE TRANSFORMATION				
WILLINGNESS	COURAGE	CURIOSITY	VULNERABILITY	TRUST

If you are willing, a little courageous, curious, vulnerable, and trust that healthier relationships, especially the one with yourself, will generate constructive transformation, then these energies can begin to start healing the parts of you that are causing you mental and emotional suffering and disempowerment. Though that suffering has kept you safe in its familiarity, it has also kept you repeating painful relationship patterns and has fed your disempowerment. Are you ready to let go of the problematic and disempowering illusions that not-love has programmed into your human operating system?

Love Ignites Peace is the journey of washing all of the not-love self-beliefs and behaviors out of your mind and replacing them with love's more evolved beliefs. As you become self-aware and clean out your not-love self-beliefs and then refresh them with more loving beliefs, you create a kinder more compassionate inner dialogue. You transform your vocabulary to include words that describe actions like understanding, forgiveness, discernment, acceptance, allowing, and respect. Love, spoken through your words, actions, and feelings builds happiness, creativity, purpose, and cooperation. Any word that nourishes the garden of goodness in your heart and in someone else's is love in action.

On an individual level, are you ready to create healthy self-beliefs that love and accept yourself just as you are? Are you ready to let go of self-judgment, self-sabotage, self-punishment, self-loathing, disappointment, lack, unworthiness, undeservingness, and not-enoughness, and to integrate self-beliefs that support your magnificence? It is okay to say that you are beautiful, smart, kind, abundant, and successful. Those qualities are the truth of who you actually are. They are self-love in action, which empowers you to break through the glass ceiling of your limitations and ignite your human potential. When you 100% know these qualities as your truth, there is no ego, only a quiet and humble inner knowing that affects how you think and speak about yourself, how you interact with others, and who/what you attract into your life.

It is up to you to adopt a self-love vocabulary. The unconditional love that you offer yourself will spill out and saturate all of your relationships. Your self-love has such a global effect that offering that love will pour from your mind as a waterfall of heart-based thoughts toward the strangers who make up your human community.

So why love? Because love is the master builder that architects all things good both for you and our human community. Love encourages you to shine your light as bright as you can make it glow. You are never too much or not enough, you are just right. Love generates happiness. You have the ability to love yourself so much that it feels like you are growing sunshine in your heart and a prolific garden of goodness in your life. Love transforms the opposite of love (not-love) into healthy and empowered relationships. It creates prosperity and harmony. It sets healthy boundaries with unhealthy people. Love says that you matter, that you are important as a person, and that you are safe. Within all of your relationships, love unifies and brings people together. Love is the most powerful energy source on the planet. Love always triumphs over not-love because love, in her purest of forms, supports and nurtures life.

Love's energy has the power to revolutionize your individual life by activating your unlimited human potential. When you entangle yourself in love's words and actions, the highest good for all is the only possible outcome.

Why love? Because love empowers the kind of change that benefits everyone, not just some.

DEFINITIONS

Love in Action
Goodness in action that fortifies your life (and all life) and encourages you and our collective human community to embody our authentic selves and to create experiences that bring us joy, freedom, and peace. It is the vocabulary that transmits the energy which says that you matter and what you want is important. It is the empowerment of living your full potential.

Not-Love
The harmful opposite of love. Words and actions laced with judgment, control, fear, manipulation, degradation,

not-enoughness, punishment, acrimony, self-righteous-ness, greed, lack, and any other word that doesn't support a person's goodness and full potential. Not-love creates hurt and is the kindling for the unhealthy and limiting self-be-liefs that you unknowingly create about yourself from your relationships and your environment. It creates disempow-erment.

Subconscious Mind

A part of your mind where mental activity occurs, but you are unconscious (unaware) of what is occurring. "Sub" means below and this mental activity is occurring just underneath your conscious mind. Your subconscious beliefs become the *code*/programming that runs your *human operating system*. The *code* (subconscious beliefs) you installed as a result of your life's experiences then generates the output your conscious thoughts, your feelings, and your behaviors. As your subconscious programs align with your human potential (love), your human operating system responds with conscious thoughts, feelings, and behaviors that match your new programming.

Human Operating System Code

Equals your subconscious beliefs.

Human Operating System

The part of your mind known as the subconscious. It stores, unbeknownst to you, the self-beliefs that act as the "code" that generates the output of your feelings and behaviors.

With every computer, the operating system is accessible and can be changed; the same principles apply to your human operating system.

Self-Beliefs
The beliefs you have accumulated about yourself based on how you interpret yourself from your relationships and the ecosystem of your environment. The self-beliefs stored in your subconscious mind act as the code for your human operating system, which determines your feelings and your behaviors.

Your Human Potential
A life free of the self-imposed limitations. A life that embodies happiness, abundance, purpose, compassion, freedom, creativity, and peace. See the Love vs Not-Love chart for a more comprehensive list of love-in-action energies that fortify your ability to live your human potential and encourage others to live theirs.

ASSIMILATING CHAPTER 2:

*What stories and questions in this chapter
reflect back to you a quality or an experience
you can identify with?*

_____

_____

_____

_____

_____

_____

_____

_____

_____

_____

_____

_____

_____

_____

_____

_____

Love Ignites Peace

_____

_____

_____

_____

_____

_____

_____

_____

_____

_____

_____

_____

_____

_____

_____

_____

_____

_____

_____

_____

_____

_____

Our Next Evolution

3
Introducing *Love's 6 Actions*

CHAPTER 3 CHALLENGE:

*Create your own list of words that describe
love in action. At the end of this chapter
is a list to get you started.*

When the Universe gives you a message like *Love Ignites Peace* it really gets you thinking about love. What is love exactly? How can I love bigger and better? How is love connected to the human experience?

Love as an action is a steady rain that washes away any and all limitations and refills every person with the freedom of living their potential. It doesn't want you to hurt, or suffer, or feel limited by fear-filled beliefs that prevent you from feeling peace and joy. Life is a game, your personal human experience, which provides challenges for your soul's growth. Love is who you innately are and your life experiences provide the obstacles that you must overcome in order to return to love.

Love Ignites Peace is love's call to action so you can progress beyond the limitations that have kept you from living as peace. As you walk the parallel path of loving yourself and loving others, self-awareness is the key that swings open the door to your ability to achieve that. It also unlocks other doors in the process, like compassion and empathy, so you can offer love as an action to everyone you meet.

The first place I had to start exploring love's unlimited powers was within myself, the most important relationship in my life. Coming to this realization wasn't ego-based or selfish, it was the only way I was going to stop living in the past. The past is where I had created the self-beliefs that were keeping me afraid, unhappy, and disempowered. I had to back out of all of the not-love beliefs that were preventing me from loving myself so that I could leave the past behind and move forward toward the future I wanted to create. It was my heart's deepest desire to become the all-things-good energy of love, which for me included but was not limited to feeling joy, embodying peace, offering compassion, responding with non-judgment, and always being kind.

Boundaries were something that I'd struggled with, and I knew the future me wanted to be love in action, but with strong personal boundaries. Sometimes we get love confused with too much self-giving and self-sacrifice. When we truly embody love of others we are able to stand in our power and offer kindness and compassion, but not at the expense of our own needs.

I knew my relationship with myself was dictating my

behaviors, my feelings, and my choices. What I longed for was to feel free from the avalanche of fears that buried me in my inability to say what I wanted to say and to take empowered action for myself. To gain deeper self-awareness I started by examining my most challenging relationship; the one that I believed was contributing the most to my unhappiness. My relationship with my husband had left me feeling victimized and corrosive with blame. "If only he would treat me with respect and kindness, I'd feel so much better," I thought.

As part of my self-discovery, I looked to thought leaders in the human development field for answers to transcending my limitations. At one of those workshops, I had an "ah-ha" moment that helped me to take responsibility for my own feelings. If I felt like a victim, I'd never be able to become the love I could feel was just waiting to be let in. By staying in the victim mentality I was only causing myself to be trapped under the glass ceiling of my disempowerment. Blame said that I wasn't responsible for our relationship, only he was. But as my self-awareness began to bloom, I realized that I shouldered just as much responsibility as he did.

In that moment, I knew I had to let go of my expectations that this person would change. I couldn't expect him to be someone different than who he was. If he wanted to change, then that journey was up to him. I understood, with my newfound self-awareness, that our individual human operating systems were both programmed with self-beliefs that were keeping us from loving ourselves and each other. If I wanted change, it was up to me to reprogram my own operating system.

I was lucky and I often say that I won the parent lottery. My parents are kind, compassionate people that taught me how to live love as an action. How they treated and interacted with me installed programs in my mind that told me I was loved and loveable. They made me believe that I was important and that I mattered. But their love couldn't shelter me from the world outside of my home. Other relationships in my life, because of the words and actions of those individuals, caused me to perceive myself as not enough, that I was a bad person who said bad things, and that I wasn't smart enough or capable enough to take care of myself.

Through the words and actions (suggestions) of others, my mind interpreted what I perceived they were telling me about me, and then I, without self-awareness, created the self-beliefs that matched those self-perceptions. My mind adopted their suggestions and unknowingly added my own interpretation to what they were telling me about me. Other people's suggestions about us, good or bad, true or not true, are so powerful that they can become reality to our self-perceiving minds.

Learning about *Love's 6 Actions* was me exploring my own human experience. What had I learned about myself from my relationships, the good and the not-so-good? What suggestions from others had I just accepted as my truth?

How was my day-today environment affecting my feelings? Every relationship, every trauma, every not-so-great memory had to be examined and explored through the lens of self-awareness.

What had that experience taught me to believe about myself? What fears had that experience unknowingly planted in my self-beliefs? This was a process of exploring my own human experiences so I could become self-aware of what was keeping me stuck. I had to examine my past so I could stop creating my life's experiences from the not-love baggage that I'd accumulated. It was a process of letting go of all the beliefs and energies that kept me limited and then taking personal responsibility for my relationship with myself and my relationships with others.

I read and studied the law of attraction, the works of Dr. Bruce Lipton, Dr. Joe Dispenza, and others. The common thread that I learned from these thought leaders is that our self-beliefs attract into our lives, like magnets, what we believe about ourselves. If you don't believe you will be successful, life will create obstacles that prevent success. If you believe you aren't worthy, then you will attract people and situations in your life that confirm that belief. Our self-beliefs are our self-fulling prophecies.

What were my relationships reflecting back to me about myself? For years I'd felt like I wasn't enough, and my most challenging relationship, the one with my husband, reflected that belief back to me through the words we exchanged. My body wasn't the right shape, I didn't exercise enough, or I ate too much. Words spoken to me held a mirror that reflected back to me what I already believed about myself. Long ago my mind had, without self-awareness, accepted the suggestion that I wasn't enough. If I had believed I was enough, then I would not have been triggered by my husband's words. Now that I am self-aware, if someone speaks to me as if I am not enough, I have clear boundaries and I am able to say, "You have no right to say those things to me. That may be your truth, but it isn't my truth about myself."

Relationships, with others and the one with yourself, can be your greatest teachers as you unlock the doors to your self-awareness.

Understanding love was a journey to self-awareness that helped me understand the limitations I'd created about myself that told me I wasn't 100% loveable. Then, that understanding prompted me to install the self-beliefs into my human operating system that told me I was 100% lovable and worthy of love's boundless goodness. I know that every bit of me and every bit of you are good, and love as an action helps us to feel that goodness coursing through our minds and our hearts.

Love as an action had me look within to find what was keeping me from feeling happy and free to be me. It was a deep examination into the relationship with me. My life has been a contemplation on how to live the words *Love Ignites*

Peace. Love's 6 Actions were the stopping points along that journey where I paused and then returned to many times for extended reflection. They address the relationship you have with yourself and they address the relationships you have with others. *Love's 6 Actions* can help you build a strong and lasting path to loving yourself, and a parallel path to loving others. You have to learn to walk both paths to truly embody the statement *Love Ignites Peace.*

Our relationships are complex and nuanced with webs of self-beliefs created from how we've interpreted ourselves from our environments, along with the entanglement of our relationships. None of us escapes this phenomenon because that is how we learned how to be ourselves. Our personalities evolve from the meanings we unknowingly create about ourselves as we interpret who we think we are based on how people are interacting with us. We create self-perceptions from how we believe other people see us and what they are saying (suggesting) to us. We interpret ourselves based on what we observe from our environment. We adopt our self-beliefs from how others treat us and how we see them treating others.

If this game of being human came with a "how the game is played" insert, this would be first and foremost in our minds; we unknowingly create who we believe we are through the interpretation of our personal experiences within our surrounding environments. No one is exempt from this process of how they embody their individuality.

Becoming self-aware is the strategic path to winning the

game. It is our job to understand ourselves so deeply that we bring the limitations of what is keeping us from loving ourselves to our awareness so it can be healed. Returning to love is how the game is won. We are all pieced together from the same rules; self-interpretation based on our relationships and our environments. However, the mental patterns we create through self-interpretation differ for all of us.

My most challenging relationship was one of the greatest gifts I've ever received, because it brought to the surface many of my self-beliefs filled with fears, which had to be overcome so I could love myself. Those beliefs were the prison bars that kept me trapped in my disempowerment. That relationship was the mirror which reflected back to me that I wasn't enough, that I was responsible for his feelings and everyone else's too, and that I believed I needed someone to control my life because I wasn't smart or capable enough to take care of myself. Our relationship magnified what was keeping me disempowered and reflected it all back to me. *Love's 6 Actions* have guided my own healing and have helped me return to self-love. They have also helped me love others, even the people that hurt me.

I wish *Love's 6 Actions* were like going through a car wash where you came out cleansed and dirt-free with just one wash, but they are mini workshops that have to be visited and revisited until you've mastered them. When you feel like you still haven't overcome the limitations keeping you from loving yourself, come back to them and meditate on their wisdom. When someone triggers you, come back to them. When you feel angry and filled with blame, come back to them. They are tributaries of insight that will all eventually flow into unconditional love's one big river.

These 6 actions are do-it-yourself practices that help you make incremental changes in offering love (action) to yourself and others. As you work with them and rework with them, they become a habit for you to lean into when you feel not-love creeping back into your mind and your emotions.

When you offer yourself and others these loving actions, you create compassion and kindness. You stand in empathy's shoes and give yourself and others grace for why they behaved the way they did. Becoming love is an infinitely patient process, so don't judge how long it takes you to master *Love's 6 Actions*. It took me 15 years, but time is irrelevant; what is important is that you are making your way back to love's unlimited goodness. Your self-growth trip to embodying *Love Ignites Peace* has its own timeline, with no judgment in the process. Giving yourself this kind of perspective is a big act of self-kindness, which is love in action.

Action denotes movement and returning to love requires a shift in perspective. Love as an action first starts in your heart as your desire to heal what has kept you limited. In order for that to happen, love as an action becomes an intellectual process, an unraveling of your mind (self-beliefs), so that you can install a more expanded perspective called wisdom. At some point in the process, after love (action) has mastered your mind, it will master your heart so you can truly feel love for yourself and for our collective human community. When your heart has mastered your mind, *Love's 6 Actions* become your lifestyle.

LOVE'S 6 ACTIONS – LOVE OF SELF
    Understand your story
    Discern instead of judge
    Allow yourself to grow through experience
    Forgive yourself because you understand
    Accept yourself
    Respect yourself and your unique journey

Understanding grows self-awareness and compassion. *Discernment* eliminates judgment's shame and blame by helping you get to the root of your disempowering beliefs. *Allowing* permits you to grow in wisdom from your life's experience and it helps you embrace life's flow. *Forgiveness* promotes freedom. *Acceptance* teaches you to love yourself exactly as you are no matter where you are in the process. *Respect* promotes your sovereign use of boundaries and the feelings of reverence for your resilience.

    Love's 6 Actions can create more love as an action in your life. They outline an internal code of conduct for you. When you practice *Love's 6 Actions* you become more self-aware of what has kept you from loving yourself. They help you to identify what needs to be healed and they bring you to those insights with compassion and empathy for what constructed your own glass ceiling. They give you the space and the time, as much time as you need, to discover your true, authentic self. Without directly asking "Who am I," they give you the leeway to grow into that answer.

Love's 6 Actions expand your self-perspective. You begin to see yourself through a different lens, one that focuses on what you need to heal in order to return to love as an action for yourself.

The only person you can change is you. The only person who can truly choose for you, is you. Victor Frankel, a Jewish psychiatrist and neurologist who survived four years in various concentration camps, said in his book, *Man's Search for Meaning*, "When we are no longer able to change a situation, we are challenged to change ourselves." Choosing to act with *Love's 6 Actions* changes you. As you change, how you perceive the people in your life changes too.

It was amazing how, as I transformed what I believed about myself, the mirror of my relationships changed, too. What once would have triggered me now has no power over me. When I let go of my need to control how the other person was acting and behaving towards me, I allowed them to have their own experience. I was able to see it as just that, an experience for both of us. My journey to learning how to love myself has been my life's greatest gift, because it taught me how to carve a path to that destination. What I offered myself, I knew I could offer to others.

Love's 6 Actions – Love of Self builds the foundation for

you to solve your problems from a new consciousness (wisdom) and live in life's unlimited freedom of joy and success. Love begins with your most important relationship, the one with yourself. And then like a field of wildflowers, it spreads and shares its beauty with everyone that passes by. Love is your innate power and *Love Ignites Peace* is the inner GPS that keeps routing you back to *Love's 6 Actions*.

LOVE'S 6 ACTIONS – LOVE OF OTHERS

Understand every person has a story

Discern instead of judge

Allow others to have their own experience

Forgive others because you understand

Accept every person as they are

Respect every person and their unique journey

Understanding that every person has a story, and that their story has influenced the self-beliefs which determine their behavior, stretches wide your arms of compassion; far enough even to embrace the people that challenge you the most. *Discerning* why a person behaves the way they do disarms judgment's anger. *Allowing* empowers you to step back and know that this person has signed up for their own set of unique experiences to grow and learn from. *Forgiveness* frees you from holding onto their limited and unhealthy baggage as your own. *Acceptance* releases your need to control the other person. *Respect* installs boundaries that keep you from rescuing, saving, or changing that person.

Love as an action brings out the best in you and encourages you to see the best in another person. When we give our attention to a person's goodness, the energy that created all of the negative feelings and emotions loses its power. If we keep treating each other with the old consciousness of self-righteousness and divisiveness, nothing will change. Those behaviors will continue to generate reactions that match them in self-awareness. Just as *Love's 6 Actions – Love of Self* provides love's internal code of conduct for interacting with yourself, *Love's 6 Actions – Love of Others* provides love's external code of conduct for interacting with others.

Love's 6 Actions neutralize negative narratives and the need to be right by encouraging thoughtful responses. They disempower conflict and promote peaceful interactions. They seek the reasons for the actions, thus deactivating blame's explosive arsenal. Unconditional love has seemed unattainable to many, but act by act, *Love's 6 Actions* can help to build a solid path to accomplishing what has previously seemed impossible.

Love's 6 Actions, when you offer them to others, build your empathy muscles. What the other person has experienced in their life, in some small or big way, connects with your experiences. Things happened to you that made you feel happy or sad. That is the same for every person in our collective human community. We've all felt the pain and hurt of not-so-nice words and actions and we can empathize with how that has felt. Empathy helps you understand the damage a person's not-love experiences have had on what they believe about themselves; because, though you've had different experiences, you too have had experiences that affect what you believe about yourself.

Unconditional love of others doesn't mean that you have to feel love for someone who hurt you or for a random stranger; however, it does means that you are able to offer every person understanding, discernment, allowing, forgiveness, acceptance, and respect as a human being. Like you, they too have a lifetime of accumulated not-love self-beliefs. As human beings we all are doing the best we can, given our hurts and our traumas in combination with our self-awareness.

There have been many people who have hurt me with their words and actions, but once I understood the wisdom contained in *Love's 6 Actions*, I became empowered to offer unconditional love to myself and to others. Unconditional love of self doesn't mean that you allow another person to hurt or harm you. Self-love responds with strong boundaries that advocate for your mental and physical wellbeing. It doesn't take responsibility for other people's actions or for their feelings, it challenges you to take responsibility for your own actions and feelings. Unconditional love is your ability to give and to receive *Love's 6 Actions* to yourself and to others.

When you interact with Love's 6 Actions, then you've mastered becoming love.

Maybe you aren't ready to open to the vulnerability needed to walk the track of self-love yet, but that doesn't mean you can't work on walking the path of loving others. Not one thing about walking the parallel paths of love of self and love of others is linear. Ironic, isn't it? I hopped back and forth for many years until I could walk with the self-awareness that allowed me to balance both tracks. Choosing to become love is a journey. It took me 15 years to transform my subconscious self-beliefs so I could truly live the words *Love Ignites Peace* as my lifestyle. It may not take as long for you, because there are so many resources out there to help you, including the ones provided by *Love Ignites Peace*. But if it does take some time, don't judge yourself for that. It takes the time it needs for you to come to understanding.

For fun, I decided to look up what the number 6 *(Love's 6 Actions)* meant in numerology, and boy did the Universe give me a gigantic wink. "The number 6 is the embodiment of the heart. It represents unconditional love and the ability to support, nurture, and heal. It is a powerful force of compassion and empathy, and its warm light is a beacon of hope. Its role is to use its heart and soul to be of service to others."[1] *Love's 6 Actions* are in service to your heart and the 8 billion hearts of our collective human community.

Love's 6 Actions, when offered to self and to others, are behaviors that generate more love. And when more love is offered more loving behaviors result. We have to be the trendsetters and take the path less followed until that path becomes a major thoroughfare for more people. The early adopters literally pave the way for others to get on board. Someone has to have the courage and the desire to create this new consciousness in order to create a better reality for our world. Why not you?

Before we explore each of *Love's 6 Actions*, there are three other parts of the human experience that merit discussion: *life as an experience*, a deeper examination of the *subconscious mind*, and *duality*. If life is a game that we are all trying to master, then understanding the purpose of our experiences and how our minds interpret those experiences within duality's challenges are important components.

DEFINITIONS:

Love's 6 Actions
An internal and external code of conduct that promotes love as an action in your relationship with yourself and with others.

Unconditional Love
Our ability to offer love as an action to yourself and others without judgment, blame, manipulation, or any other not-love action or condition. *Love's 6 Actions* in action.

EXERCISE:

In the chart below are words that describe love as an action. The energy of these words are part of *Love's 6 Actions*. Add your own words to this list, as there are many more words that characterize love as an action.

ENERGIES THAT IGNITE TRANSFORMATION			
KINDNESS	COMPASSION	ACCEPTANCE	WELCOMING
PATIENCE	EMPATHY	ALLOWING	CARING
DISCERNMENT	FLOW	FORGIVENESS	CONCERN
EQUALITY	WORTHY	FREEDOM	WELL-BEING
COOPERATION	ENOUGH	SUPPORT	BOUNDARIES
COLLABORATION	HIGHEST GOOD	HEAL	GRACE
GOODNESS	SAFETY	UNDERSTANDING	POSITIVITY
NURTURE	TRUST	HEART	HOPE
SERVICE	SUCCESS	DESERVING	RESILIENCE

4

We Are All Here To Have Experiences

QUESTIONS FOR CONTEMPLATION AS YOU
DIGEST CHAPTER 4:

Which of your relationships challenge you the most?
What are the impactful life experiences that
you are here to grow and evolve beyond?

There are many things we humans have in common, and one of those is that we are all here to learn through our experiences. That may seem obvious, but it is through experience that our consciousness (self-awareness) evolves. Some of us have chosen a very difficult set of experiences to evolve beyond, and others have chosen a less intense set. We don't often think about the possibility that we are a soul first and a physical being enlivened by that soul.

Many years of my self-discovery have been spent studying the information contained in my soul's choices. When I realized my true nature is that I am a spiritual being having a human experience, the pieces which had been puzzling me started fitting into places I previously couldn't see.

It took me from seeing my life through a tunnel to being at a 30,000-foot elevation where I could observe the entire landscape of my life.

Based on what I have learned, before I was born my soul signed up for a set of purposeful experiences. The people in my life were the supporting actors who played the roles that my soul needed to have that experience. When you look at your life as a game, this is the game's challenge; to return to love through a complicated combination of experiences. When you are born you stand at the entrance to your life, and as you take your first breaths, through self-perceptions, you unknowingly start creating your experiences— your life's personal maze. The people in your life and your environment all support the experiences your soul has chosen.

The experience I was here to overcome was to return to my full power. That meant being able to speak my truth and stand up for myself, and to learn how to do that with love of self and love of others. There were many smaller experiences within the larger experience; I had to overcome oceans of self-distrust and self-doubt.

Many years ago, I treated myself to a reading with a Vedic astrologer, and he told me that the primary karma I was here to transcend was self-punishment. His message to me knocked me conscious. I could see how I'd been punishing myself with my choices. In junior high, a friend's mom who bullied me, arrived at my house with the specific intention of punishing me for what I'd said. I kept punishing myself throughout my life for saying something bad and by making choices that set me up for more punishment.

My most challenging relationship, my husband, punished me with his words and actions. From trying to get me fired from my job to telling me that no one liked me and I didn't deserve friends, I allowed him to punish me for being me; I was incapable of standing up for myself and I was afraid I wasn't capable of taking care of myself. I let fear lead my choices because I didn't love myself enough to leave. None of us are exempt from life's challenges because our souls have all chosen a set of experiences that we must overcome.

I don't know what my husband signed up for as his soul's experience. To give me what my soul desired, I know he signed up for a difficult human experience. His childhood was filled with his father's anger and resentment at having the additional responsibility of children. His father had worked since he was 5 years old, and having children just added another burden to his already heavy suitcase. From one to another, they passed down their soul's experiences, as they perceived themselves within their relationship. My husband didn't want to become his father, but because his human operating system was programmed with feeling so much not-love and rejection, he became his own unique version of his father's behaviors.

I feel unconditional love and gratitude for him, that his soul agreed to such a difficult childhood so he could play the role for my soul's desired experience. His soul's choices enabled my soul's chosen experience. For his soul to agree to this he had to feel a great love for me. He agreed to a difficult path for my benefit. This is not to say that whatever he agreed upon for me was singularly for my benefit; his choices also created a path of great learning and evolution for his own soul. Though we chose very different experiences, our souls, through great love for each other, traveled a parallel soul/human journey together, with our souls mirroring for each other what the other needed in order to grow through experience into self-love.

Awareness of the choices your soul makes for your soul/human journey activates your human consciousness (awareness and perspective) into the expanded possibility of greater self-love and compassion. This, in turn, expands your ability to offer that same energy to others.

My spouse's soul chose a kind but passive mother and an angry father. The parents my soul chose were loving people. For most of my life, decision making for me was very difficult. I felt like pollen in the wind, not knowing what direction I should go, so I gave up and let the wind take me wherever it thought best. My mom acted as the wind in my early life, making decisions for me so I didn't have to do it myself. Because of the role she, and sometimes my dad, played for me, I'd conditioned myself to believe that

I needed to be taken care of by a stronger, more decisive personality—someone who could make the decisions I was incapable of making.

My husband was conditioned through his upbringing that it was him against the world. He developed an unwavering inner strength and determination that forged an inner compass that always pointed him in the right direction. In his mind, that direction was not only correct for him but absolutely right regardless of others' circumstances or view of the world. When he and I met, we were like magnets, unable to stop the pull of our being together. I needed his strength and decisiveness, and he needed to be loved. I knew how to love, as I'd been raised with tremendous love. I believed I could love him enough to soften his sharp edges, and he felt he could mold me into whatever he believed was right.

We were opposite edges of the same energies. His need for love and my ability to love him regardless, along with the strength of his inner compass and my broken inner compass, were constantly seeking balance, but we were always out of sync.

The majority of us are average, normal, mostly healthy people. We go to work, we have families and friends, we travel and play. We weren't born with something devastating that makes negotiating the world a bit more challenging. You might be asking yourself "What could my soul have possibly chosen to bring to this soul/human experience?"

None of us live perfect lives filled with unconditional love and joy all of the time. In fact, most of us rarely live that way. By taking a deep look at your relationships through the lens of *What did my soul come here to learn,* the puzzle pieces of your own soul's choices will begin to emerge. Deep self-awareness promotes personal evolution and your ability to live *Love's 6 Actions.*

Let's imagine some examples of this. What if your mother or father never told you they loved you? How has their lack of using these words made you feel about yourself? Those *feelings contain the nuggets* your soul really wants you to uncover. Possibly, the lack of those words and your other interactions with your mother or father left you feeling like you could never do or be enough for anyone. So you spent your life being a perfectionist at everything in the unconscious hope that you'd finally be recognized as loveable, or even just recognized as a valuable human being.

What if one of your parents was constantly critical of everything you said and did? You could never please that parent. You unconsciously felt that you as a person were fundamentally unpleasing to everyone. You created ways to hide yourself away from the world, so you didn't have to unconsciously feel the criticisms of others, real or imagined.

What if your father acted unpredictably, directing his fury at you when least expected? What if your family and friends dismissed your opinions and accomplishments? What if you couldn't say what you wanted to say with certain people? What if you were raised very poor or very rich? Both energies carry their unique challenges and opportunities for your soul's evolution. Having money does not mean your soul has evolved back to knowing itself. In fact, money in general, whether you have a lot or a little, offers many lessons.

What if you were adopted? What if you felt abandoned by your family or even your friends? What if your parents were complete overachievers with extraordinarily high expectations for you? What if as a child you were more of a parent to your parent than your parent was to you? What if your parent was an alcoholic, suffered addiction, or was mentally ill? What if you were physically, verbally, or sexually abused? What if your parents were kind and loving, and yet you still can't fully love yourself?

The learning is found when you uncover how that chosen experience made you feel about yourself. Listen to the words you speak about yourself and others. Those words contain your feelings, and your self-beliefs are hidden behind your feelings. The things you find most annoying about others are the mirrors reflecting back to you what you really believe about yourself. You can then review that information from the mountain top of expanded wisdom and begin looking at your life from the panoramic view of your soul's chosen experiences.

Siblings raised in the same household with the same parents never react to their parents the same way, nor do they assimilate their parents conditioning the same way. I loved it when my parents, especially my mom, made my decisions because I already felt powerless to make the right decision on my own. My sister, on the other hand, detested my mom making decisions for her. My sister's soul desired to experience freedom of expression and independence. Therefore, the same parent, acting the same way with each child, created a different experience for both of us, because our souls' desired different experiences. The same for my spouse's siblings. They all lived with the same angry father, but each of them reacted differently to his anger.

Your soul chooses its parents, because that is usually the structural relationship which constructs your own unique foundation for how you feel about yourself and how you interact within all other relationships. My parents provided me with the foundation of unconditional love so that I knew what unconditional love felt like. They also unknowingly empowered my feelings of disempowerment by taking extraordinary care of me. My mom dressed me with her impeccable taste for clothes. So how I dressed was my mom's gift being reflected into the world, not me reflecting me. People would complement me on my outfits, but inside I knew I was an imposter being recognized for someone else's genius. My every need was taken care of and I was left with little responsibility other than school, extra-curricular activities, and play.

All of these things my parents did out of complete

unconditional love, and very possibly because of our souls' agreement with each other. Their actions nurtured my soul's desired experience and set me up for the perfect relationship to augment my powerlessness, my marriage. It also set me up to bring the message of *Love Ignites Peace* to the world, because they showed me love in its infinite expressions.

Like me, you chose many relationships that reinforce the experiences your soul desires. Like a layered cake with a variety of cake flavors, your soul creates your life by layering its choices into one cohesive cake, held together by the frosting of your physical life in human form. Choosing your relationships are but one flavor of the many flavor choices that your soul makes before incarnating into physical form.

Your soul chose different cultural and socio-economic challenges, and a particular vehicle (body) from which to experience those challenges. Think of your body like a vehicle. Your soul chose a vehicle (body), and a variety of other preferences. You see the world differently if you are driving a convertible through the Pyrenees versus an army tank through the desert—the vehicle itself and its locale determine the experience you will have.

Our physical bodies have evolved into infinite choices of make, model, size, color, and after-market accessories. Your unique body/vehicle becomes a layer of your soul's choices. Your soul also chose a culture and geographic part of the world, a gender (or not), and a sexual preference. Each of these choices layer your soul/human lifetime with different conditions and cultural structures, creating specific containers for self-exploration.

You might have chosen to be an Indian man with a deformity; the color of your skin, your culture, and the deformity, supporting the experience of being poor and shunned. Or you might have chosen to be an extraordinarily beautiful dark-skinned woman, your beauty and skin color affecting how you are treated by others and how you treat others in return. Or you might have chosen to be transgendered, trying to express yourself and your feelings among a sea of judgment and cultural backlash. Possibly you chose to be very short or very tall, sickly or healthy, obese or stick thin, attractive or unattractive, rich, poor, or middle class, straight or gay or somewhere in-between, Hindu or Jewish; the list goes on in an infinite number of combinations.

Your human body fortifies your soul's desire for growth and evolution. All of these potential combinations of choices contain *information* about what your soul selected for your soul/ human journey. It's up to you to begin asking what your soul is here to learn, so you can learn it, move beyond it and evolve.

Like an acorn seed produces an oak tree, your human seed contains the genetic information for you. The acorn contains all the information about the tree so it can grow into an oak, not a piñon tree, not a willow tree. Your genetic information tells your cells to create a human body with certain physical characteristics and personality traits. Like the tree, the physical you lives in an environment that supports its growth, but the specific condition of every tree varies, which determines how it actually grows.

Your environment, defined as the totality of your personal relationships, your body vehicle, your culture/location, your religious upbringing, and your socio-economic status, supports your soul's choices for desired growth. This contributes to how the whole of you grows—physically, mentally, emotionally, and spiritually. Your soul's choices align with your genetic choices, creating your interactive, combined soul/human life.

When we incarnate, as part of our evolutionary curriculum, our soul forgets who it truly is—love. As our soul enters our body, it separates itself from the unconditional love of source energy, suffering amnesia of its true identity. One of our human ego's roles is to disrupt the knowing of our true, made-from-love self. It assists by masking your soul's memory from your human consciousness. The purpose of our soul's journey through a vast and infinite combination of experiences is to cultivate compassion and unconditional love in order to reunite with love as our ultimate power source. It's important that we take a moment and feel compassion toward ourselves and others for the challenging choices we've all made. Though we feel like we are separate from each other, it is through our soul's love that we've all chosen to have this human experience together.

The avatars, mystics, and yogis, through their messages and in the language of their time, were all trying to help humanity receive this message and move beyond the immense suffering that humanity has created and perpetuated. Causing suffering in ourselves and others doesn't bring us closer to salvation. Salvation materializes from our own efforts to transcend our need to suffer and to cause suffering for others. Suffering breeds chaos, anger, hate, greed, and fear—the language of not-love and the destroyers of peace. Suffering generates more suffering. Only love empowers more love, lighting our way to peace, abundance, and joy. Understanding the experiences our souls choose illuminates our path to eliminating our mental and emotional suffering, so that we can find unconditional love for ourselves and others.

If we are souls first, it matters not what vehicle or belief system we choose when we arrive, because we are ultimately all the same. Our unique soul, and the unique souls of our collective human community unify us. First, we must know and see this reality within ourselves; then we can know and see that reality in others. As we discover our unique soul, we begin to comprehend that we are souls first, and our soul has masterminded our experiences. From there we can increase our awareness about our challenges and master them. Changing our perceptions changes our beliefs, which ultimately changes our human consciousness.

Those new perceptions encourage compassion
because we begin to understand that every single

*human on this planet is attempting to do the same
thing—to master being an ever-evolving soul,
experiencing life in a unique human body.*

Digging into our pasts can feel daunting, and sometimes we just don't feel like we have the courage to do that, but when we detach as much as we can from the emotions of those painful memories and look at the experiences as *information*, we can more easily start unraveling those experiences through questioning.

How did I perceive myself from that experience? How did I interpret myself from that interaction? What lesson was there for me to learn from that experience? These questions give us a starting point regarding the experiences that we are here to overcome. Instead of looking at our lives as stagnant, unbending realities, we understand that as humans we are all here creating experiences for each other. With this awareness we can gain the *information* needed to evolve beyond those experiences, if we choose.

When I looked at my life experiences individually, I could see patterns emerging. In kindergarten a teacher punished me for not following directions. That may sound trivial, but because I still remembered that moment at 45 years old, I knew there was important information about myself I needed to examine. I reflected on that experience and asked, *How did I interpret myself from that interaction? What were the meanings that I created while I was being punished in front of my classmates?*

After I asked these questions, I realized my perceptions had caused me to feel shame. My teacher's punishment hurt, mentally and physically, and filled me with embarrassment. I shut down my creativity, and in that moment I started to believe I wasn't smart enough to follow directions.

Next, I went through my important relationships and asked, *What did I learn from them about myself? How did the experiences from my childhood affect what I believed about myself?* My parents are compassionate and attentive caregivers. They took the best care of me. As a child I only needed two pairs of underwear; the one I was wearing and the one my mom was washing and would have back in my dresser drawer before 9am. My dad came to my rescue when the speech that I was writing for graduation added up to zero words. All of this was done for me with so much love. Reflecting back on these experiences, I realized that at some point I started to believe I couldn't take care of myself, because pretty much everything was done for me.

There was the big trauma that I experienced in junior high, when a friend's mother exploded with anger at me for saying something she didn't like. She was so unhappy with me, that she showed up at my house with an entourage of people and proceeded to punish the 12-year-old me with her bully-like anger. Again I asked, *What did I learn about myself from this experience? How did my 12-year-old psyche interpret herself from that interaction?*

This is the moment I remember becoming fully responsible for other people's feelings. Their feelings were my fault. I was always to blame. I no longer felt safe to say what I wanted to say. A gigantic distrust in myself and the words I spoke grew deep roots into my self-beliefs. As I've really dug into this traumatizing experience, I also discovered that I unknowingly adopted the belief that I deserved to be punished for what I said.

As I've reflected on those experiences and many more, I could see how I had attracted into my life people that blamed me for their experience. I was an easy target for them to dump their feelings into, making me feel responsible. My inability to say what I wanted to say to the people that hurt me settled like an iceberg in my throat. Standing up for myself, when people were angry at me, felt impossible to me. When I really started laying out my life experiences and looking at the information within them, I actually laughed at the fact that it was profusely bleeding gums (from within my mouth where my voice came from) that was my health crisis. Was I so verbally disempowered that my body was giving me a message? I believe the answer was unequivocally, yes.

By looking back at my life experiences through the lens of self-information, I uncovered my biggest fear; I believed I wasn't smart, creative, or capable enough to take care of myself. Therefore, when I was seeking my romantic partner, I was always looking for someone who I believed was smarter than me, more creative than me, and who I could rely on to make the decisions, because I certainly couldn't be trusted to do that. My not-love self-beliefs seeped into my choices, and from a place of disempowerment, I looked to someone else to plug the leaks of my not-love self-beliefs.

I became my story, because it was through my story that I learned how to be me. For me, the experiences from my story that I was here to overcome included: taking back my power, learning how to create strong personal boundaries, standing up for myself, and saying what I wanted to say. I imagined transforming into my authentic self, twirling with freedom and cartwheeling with joy. The information about how I learned to feel afraid and disempowered was all there from my experiences, just waiting for me to uncover the meanings that I'd subconsciously created about myself. And then I could learn to evolve beyond them. Through our soul's choices and the fact that we create who we are in relationship with each other, we share our individual experiences as a collective human community.

It is through self-awareness that we can begin to understand the information contained in our life's experiences. This awareness removes us from a claustrophobic tunnel, taking us into an expanded perspective of our life. Blame and victimhood start to lose their significance. Discernment and forgiveness become easier. Allowing and accepting feel like natural energies to offer. Your understanding muscles grow strong with empathy. All of this adds up to respect; another parallel path of offering ourselves respect for what we've experienced, and respect for others for what they've experienced. If we are all here creating experiences for each other, then why do we need to get angry? Most importantly, let's stop blaming and start interacting with *Love's 6 Actions*. *Love Ignites Peace* is the north star that will guide us out of the past and into the future that our individual and collective hearts' desire—love.

ASSIMILATING CHAPTER 4:

Which of your relationships challenge you the most? What are the impactful life experiences that you are here to grow and evolve beyond?

_____

_____

_____

_____

_____

_____

_____

_____

_____

_____

Love Ignites Peace

_____

_____

_____

_____

_____

_____

_____

_____

_____

_____

_____

_____

_____

_____

_____

_____

_____

_____

Our Next Evolution

Love Ignites Peace

_____

_____

_____

_____

_____

_____

_____

_____

_____

_____

_____

_____

_____

_____

_____

_____

_____

_____

_____

_____

_____

5

Your Subconscious Mind

QUESTIONS FOR CONTEMPLATION
AS YOU DIGEST CHAPTER 5:

Do you see yourself in any of the subconscious
programs that I list? Which ones? How have they
manifested as your feelings, emotions and behaviors?
What relationship patterns have they attracted
into your life? How are these programs connected
to your most challenging relationships?

You were already introduced to the subconscious mind in chapter 2 (please revisit the definitions for chapter 2 as you lean into this chapter); but, because it is such a powerful part of overcoming what prevents you from loving yourself and others, it merits further explanation. Your subconscious mind, how you view yourself, others, and life in general, reflects your disposition, your attitudes, and your feelings. Is your glass half full or half empty? Are you always waiting for the other shoe to drop? Do you long for financial freedom, but sit consumed in jealousy for those that have more than you? Is someone else consistently to blame for the problems that you are experiencing? Are you moments away from closing the big deal and then you self-sabotage? Do you want to feel joy, but you just can't muster your enjoyment? All of the answers to these questions are sitting in your subconscious mind.

Understanding how that secret subconscious information has been influencing your thoughts, your feelings, your behaviors, and the relationships that you attract into your life can profoundly change your mind. It is said that a person has thousands, potentially even up to 70,000, thoughts per day, and many of those thoughts are the same ones cycling over and over. Identifying and then releasing the not-love subconscious programs that are influencing those thousands of thoughts gets rid of the turbulence that has kept your mind chaotically regurgitating the same unhelpful information over and over. It turns down the volume on the disruptive and unhelpful static and turns up the volume on calm and peaceful.

If life and mastering love is a game, then your subconscious mind is another big challenge within that game. Your subconscious mind is where you store the self-beliefs you unknowingly created about yourself from all of your *experiences*. Those secret self-beliefs then influence your conscious mind; the you that shows up in the world.

Altering the data stored in your subconscious mind
is the ultimate mindset shift, because the not-love

self-beliefs that are stored in your subconscious
mind contribute to the beliefs that influence your
conscious mind and all of its associated thoughts
and feelings.

Sigmund Freud used the image of an iceberg to describe the different levels of your mind. The tip of the iceberg that sits above the water-line represents your conscious mind, the 5% to 10% of yourself that logically, rationally, creatively, and with purpose participates in life. The second level is the pre-conscious mind that sits slightly below the waterline. You aren't conscious of all of your memories at one time, but if you were asked what you did last weekend you would dip into that pre-conscious part of your mind and bring that memory to your conscious mind.[2] I discovered my personal not-love self-beliefs in the pre-conscious part of my mind, just below my conscious awareness.

It was a process of bringing those beliefs up from below the water-line to my conscious mind; thus, I refer to them as my subconscious programs. That means that they are accessible. You can dive in and discover them, if you choose. The unseen part of the iceberg, the preconscious and the unconscious mind, are the gigantic parts, the remaining 90% to 95% that sit underwater, submerged from your conscious mind. Sub means below and this part of your mind sits below your conscious awareness.

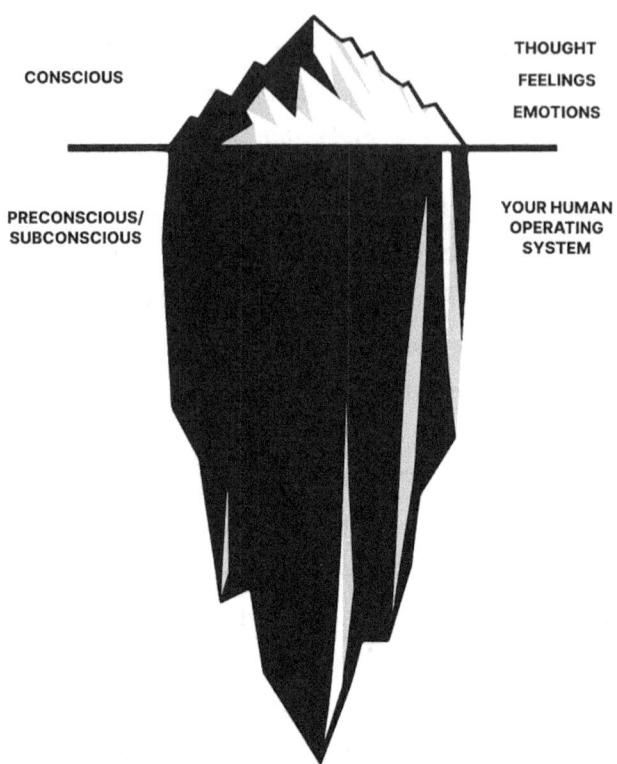

CONSCIOUS

THOUGHT
FEELINGS
EMOTIONS

PRECONSCIOUS/
SUBCONSCIOUS

YOUR HUMAN
OPERATING
SYSTEM

So what are the differences between your conscious and subconscious mind? Your conscious mind is your current awareness. It contains your wishes and your desires; your thoughts and your feelings. It works out your life with logic and rational thinking. Your conscious mind labels everything so that all of life's parts and pieces make sense. It is the self that you and others know and love.

Your subconscious mind on the other hand can be irrational, because it is based on inner experience rather than fact. It tells you that you are worthy of love and not worthy of love, enough and not enough, deserving and not deserving, all at the same time. It accepts the power of suggestion as truth. For example, a parent or a teacher told you that you'd never amount to anything. Or a doctor told you that your disease was incurable. Your subconscious mind, without logic or questioning, accepts that suggestion as is, and then inserts it as another piece of code into your human operating system. The subconscious mind feeds your habits and your judgments. It influences your behaviors, your emotions, and your long-term feelings. It is the database that holds all of the meanings you unknowingly created about yourself that you replay over and over as the patterns that show up in your life. It is where you stash the remaining bits of information that don't make your 5% to 10% conscious cut.

Years ago, my teenage daughter convinced me to go to a presentation on the subconscious mind given by a woman who, through her own personal experiences and work as a hypnotherapist, created a modality that helps you identify your subconscious programming, and then clear/release the programs that are keeping you limited and unable to fully love yourself and others. *(Information on this technique can be found at LoveIgnitesPeace.com/Our-Next-Evolution-Book.)* As I listened and learned, my intuition vibrated with a knowing that this work was important.

Somewhere deep inside of me I knew this was another important awakening encouraging me to pay attention.

The work I did with her woke me up to the ghostwriter of my subconscious mind, and profoundly transformed the conscious me who shows up as the creator of my life. Once these limiting programs were cleared, the chaos of my not-love mental chatter dissipated, reordering my self-beliefs so I could begin to feel the love that says that I matter, I am important, enough, and significant just because I am me.

As she helped me reveal the *code* that I had unknowingly written into my subconscious human operating system, I started to understand the separation between my conscious desires and the relationships that I was attracting in my life. The habits that kept me safe, disempowered, and limited were the not-love subconscious beliefs that were controlling my conscious mind. My conscious mind desired happiness and peace, but my subconscious mind was filled with self-beliefs that conflicted with what I said I wanted.

How could I feel peace when my subconscious mind believed that I constantly had to prove that I was enough for myself and those that loved me? My conscious mind said I wanted to speak my truth and to be empowered, but my subconscious mind was filled with self-beliefs that kept me afraid to say what I wanted to say.

How could I say what I wanted to say when my subconscious beliefs told me that I wasn't lovable unless I was pacifying and pleasing? In fact, some of those subconscious self-beliefs were so powerful that certain triggers would cause my physical body to react with fear-induced adrenaline, which made my ears buzz and my heart beat fast. There was a raging river that separated my conscious mind and my subconscious mind. What I consciously knew was a logical and empowered reaction couldn't take form because of the meanings I'd created about myself from my relationships, my traumas, my religious upbringing, my culture, and my environment; the sum total of my life's experiences.

My subconscious programming was overriding my ability to advocate for myself and to feel happy, which is what I consciously wanted. It was up to me to go drain that river and discover the self-beliefs that were obstructing what I consciously wanted.

Learning this work opened my mind to how the subconscious mind mostly operates our daily lives. As I interpreted myself from my life's experiences, I had secretly written the subconscious *code* that triggered my irrational, can't-speak-my-truth, fear-induced behavior—my conscious responses.

When those not-love programs were gone, my thoughts and my feelings transformed into knowing that I was enough and that I was safe to say what I wanted to say. I was able to set healthy boundaries with my unhealthy relationships. No longer was I responsible for everyone's feelings. As the not-love programs that fed my disempowerment were brought to the surface and then released, love's all-things-good energies were automatically installed.

After being introduced to my subconscious mind and reflecting back to Freud's iceberg metaphor, my mind was blown when I realized that I only was conscious of 5% to 10% of myself. What on earth was stored in that other 90% to 95% of my mind? That was a lot of myself just waiting to be discovered.

The conscious mind and the subconscious mind, because of their very different functions, seem like two separate minds, but they are part of your one mind. They function differently, but work in perfect harmony to create YOU.

None of us receives an email or an instruction manual that explains the process of how we learn to become ourselves. Nor did our parents have training on how the programming of our subconscious mind works. A baby's mind is a blank slate that begins interpreting itself from what it is happening around them. Some believe this process begins in utero.

The sum total of your experiences, including the influential people in your life (both the positive and the negative), the culture of your home, your school, your work, your societal influences, and your religious upbringing, directly influence the meanings that you created about yourself. You believe differently than your neighbor or your siblings, because your interpretations of your experiences were not exactly the same. The sum total of your life's experiences are the templates that your subconscious uses to write your story, some parts true and some not true, about who you believe yourself to be.

Our Next Evolution

*Your mind is how you know yourself. It creates
and differentiates you, the unique individual
within the collective human community.*

Our developing brains, from birth to age 2 exhibit delta waves, and then from ages 2 to 6, theta brainwaves.[3] We develop our earliest self-perceptions from a state similar to hypnosis, a not quite fully awake, yet a very receptive state, which makes it difficult to discern what is real and what is not. Our highly impressionable little minds are unable to distinguish between reality and imagination. We are open and completely receptive to all the stimuli our environment exposes us to.

This hypnotic state of mind is how we, as little sponges, first start to create subconscious meanings about ourselves, which, through our own perceptions, tells us who we think we are within the dynamic of our circumstances. Because there was so much information for your mind to make sense of, you became all of it, the good and the not-so-good. Your mind knows no boundaries; it unknowingly creates a yin and yang of self-beliefs that it stores in watery depths of your subconscious mind without your awareness.

My conscious mind knew my parents loved me and that I was worthy of love; but my subconscious believed I deserved punishment, wasn't enough, couldn't trust myself, and would be liked or loved more if I sacrificed myself to please them. Once I started really going deep, it was unbelievable how many self-limitations I'd accumulated. Some were cultural, some were connected to religious paradigms, and most were very personal; but they were all there, just waiting for me to discover them.

Culture, my teachers, my friends, and my family all had expectations of who I should be and how I should act. Meeting or not meeting those expectations gave my mind more opportunities to create meanings about myself from all of their voices. I was a girl. How is a girl in the 70's and 80's supposed to be, to look, and to act? I was a friend. What kind of friend was I supposed to be? I was a daughter, a sister, and a granddaughter. How did I measure up to my family's expectations? I was a student. What did my teachers think of me? I was supposed to be a Christian. Were my actions aligned with those teachings?

Looking at the roles I played and evaluating myself from how I thought I was meeting all of these various expectations gave me a window into the self-beliefs that I'd unknowingly recorded in my subconscious mind. The sum total of your life's experiences is punctuated by your dramas, your cast of characters, the environments in which you lived, learned, and worked, your religious training and your culture and all of their associated environments. From these influences you write your story; a narrative that contains the hidden meanings that you've unknowingly created about yourself from your experiences.

I had written my story with almost complete unawareness. I consciously knew what had happened to me, but I was oblivious to the meanings I'd written about myself from my experiences. My mind digested all of that external input and then I unknowingly turned those perceptions into my top-secret self-beliefs, which unbeknownst to me I stored in my subconscious mind. Those subconscious beliefs became my human operating system which formulated my conscious mind with all of my associated thoughts, feelings, and emotions.

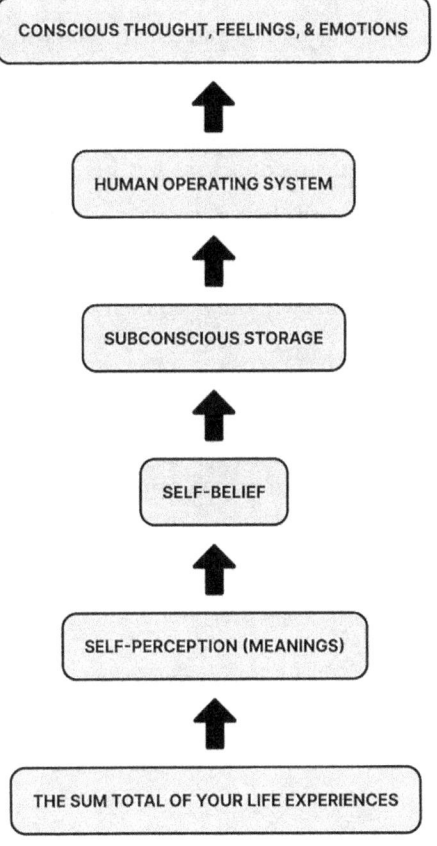

Imagine your subconscious mind like a dusty and dark warehouse with rows and rows of deep and crowded shelves, filled with your mental artifacts. Those bygone relics from your life's experiences contain the meanings you created about yourself from your self-perceptions. Those meanings turn into your secret self-beliefs, which influence your personality and trigger your reactions.

Another analogy to help you visualize how the subconscious mind works is to compare it to seeds that grow deep roots and produce fruit. When a tiny seed is embedded in the soil, you can't see the seed or what is transpiring biologically. That seed, as a subconscious self-belief, grows deep into the dirt's darkness and then it grows a plant that pushes out from the dirt as your conscious self. You can see the fruits of the seed, but you don't see the seed or root structure that has caused that plant to grow.

The billions of bits of information you process daily without awareness become the seeds you plant in the deep, dark soil of your subconscious mind. Those seeds grow into your personality and all of its associated behaviors, ultimately influencing how you respond to life.

YOU

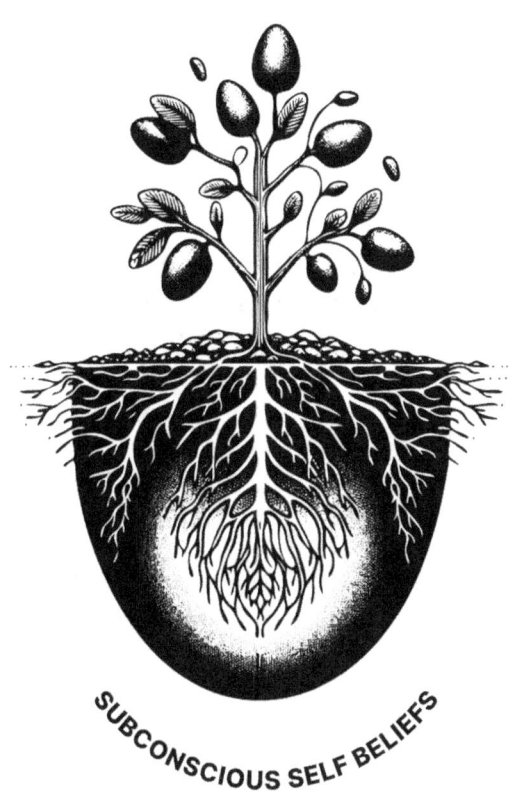

SUBCONSCIOUS SELF BELIEFS

It was the voices of my antagonists that were the most harmful to how my mind perceived myself. Some voices were intentionally destructive to me, and other antagonists meant no harm. Like a Jackson Pollack painting, they splattered their own story onto the canvas of my story, and left splashes of their colors and patterns, which then became a part of the picture I painted about myself. That is, until I became self-aware. I interpreted myself as I believed my heroes and my antagonists saw me. Long after their actual voices faded away, my subconscious mind still carried the love and the hurt that I'd absorbed, thus, perpetuating both my love and not-love self-beliefs.

Mrs. Martin was one of my story's first memorable antagonists. Kindergarten was really my first solo adventure out into the world. My cast of characters grew as my tiny feet climbed the steps of the yellow school bus and I looked into the faces of strangers. I didn't like going to school, at least not that first year, because fear (lack of safety) was my closest companion.

Mrs. Martin was fabricated from the hard times of the Depression and World Wars. It was 1971 and her face was mapped with highways that told the story of her difficult and long life. The corners of her mouth mostly pointed downwards. She managed her 5-year-old students like recruits; with discipline. When one of us got out of line, she would thump us on the head, a swift smack, usually two or more, launched from her thumb to her first finger.

The first few months of basic kindergarten training, I threw up every day. The adults thought I couldn't digest the carton of milk I was required to drink, but that wasn't the case. I was afraid because I felt unsafe. My mind was telling my little body that this was too much for me to stomach. I was terrified of the big world that no longer felt fun and safe, and I was afraid of her.

Mrs. Martin wasn't unkind to me, but there was no gentleness in her actions, nor was there any patience, especially if she thought her students were out of line. The environment of her classroom was based on punishment, not positive reinforcement and love. Avoiding a collision between her fingers and my head was my number one priority. I made it until December.

Even now I can remember the day. A winter gloom had clouded our classroom with potential snow. Christmas was approaching, and Mrs. Martin had tasked us with cutting out snowmen to decorate the walls. She showed us how to fold the paper and the draw only half of the snowman on one side. As she was talking, I could already feel my body humming with anxiety. I didn't understand and I was too afraid to ask. How do I fold the paper? How do I draw the snowman? Directionless and deaf with worry, my fingers slipped into the round-nosed, silver scissors and began to cut. My snowman was a disaster, an undefinable mess of white pieces.

I have no recollection of the words that she spoke to me as the force of her first finger connected several times with my head. Fear and shame clung to me from the inside out as I was publicly punished for something I had created. My ears buzzed and my stomach felt sick as tears dampened the white mess on my desk.

You may think this seems like a trivial story about a little girl who got in trouble for incorrectly cutting out a snowman, but as I've studied this memory, starting with how I felt and then comparing that moment with my life's patterns, what I uncovered was one of the starting points from which my squadron of not-love subconscious self-beliefs started to land.

- *I can't follow directions.*
- *I can't be trusted to get it right.*
- *I can't trust my self-expression.*
- *I am not smart enough.*
- *I am not safe.*
- *It is not safe to get it wrong.*
- *It is not safe to make a mistake.*
- *I am bad.*
- *I deserve to be punished for what I create.*
- *I don't have what it takes.*
- *I am inadequate.*

Mrs. Martin's words and actions had hurt me, and then I proceeded to hurt myself by unknowingly writing meanings into my subconscious mind that fed my disempowerment instead of my potential. From the words of my antagonists, my subconscious mind then became my long-term antagonist by writing these limiting self-beliefs as the code that was operating my day-to-day conscious self. As a result, those beliefs influenced my actions, my decisions, my thoughts, and my feelings. They made ordinary moments feel stressful. Standardized testing, filling out forms, listening to or reading directions, or any creative project, filled my ears with anxiety-filled droning.

Another antagonist from my past that profoundly impacted the not-love self-beliefs that I inserted in my subconscious mind was Suzanne Albertelli, the mother of one of my junior high school friends. On an ordinary Saturday night, the phone rang; it was my friend calling to tell me that her mom was coming to my house. Apparently, I'd said something that her mom needed to talk to me about. Fifteen minutes later a wild-eyed and sobbing Mrs. Albertelli stomped into my house, tears pouring from her tortured face. As she stepped inside the front door, she balled her words into fists and began punching my 12-year-old psyche. My parents happened to be out for dinner, so it was just me and another 12-year-old friend who was spending the night that let Mrs. Albertelli and her entourage into my house.

It had gotten back to Mrs. Albertelli that I had said her daughter Amy would be the first to get pregnant. Mrs. Albertelli was crazed and irate. "Did you say it?" she demanded. Fear flooded my body, my ears rang, and anxiety shook my hands. My wild-eyed shock and sobbing now mirrored Mrs. Albertelli's. Anxiety shut down my ability to think. Had I said it? I couldn't think, I couldn't remember. There was no fight in me, only fear. "Yes, I said it." "I am sorry." "I meant no harm."

Time stopped as I experienced this trauma. This surprise attack had come out of nowhere. I can still see Mrs. Albertelli sitting in the middle of our yellow and cream nubbed couch with her husband to her left and Amy to her right. My judge and her jury, as I sat across from them in a single wing-back chair absorbing the blows. I'd never experienced rage directed at me like that. My words had led to a severe punishment of me by someone else's parent. My parents came home not too long after they'd all arrived, astonished and dazed and trying to catch up with what was happening and who had said what; their arrival was too late to protect me from Mrs. Albertelli's verbal assault.

This was something new, and like a wounded animal, the pain was so great that I wished for death. I went to bed that night, tear-stained and drowning in shame, embarrassment, and guilt. Somehow, I'd have to go to school on Monday and face everyone, knowing that terrible thing I'd said and the punishment that Mrs. Albertelli had dispensed. Others would find out and my fall into humiliation would be complete.

As I laid my head on my pillow, I tried not to feel all the emotions from that moment; they just hurt too much. I metaphorically left my body, because the emotional pain was too much for me to physically endure. Your life experiences are filled with influential characters, the heroes and the antagonists that have come in and out of your life. Mrs. Albertelli's hostile behavior toward me lasted less than one hour, but it left me with decades of shame and self-distrust to sort through. The secret subconscious self-beliefs that I'd created from the seeds of her words took root and grew me into a teenager and then a woman who emotionally disengaged when not-love words were directed at her. She struggled to say what she wanted to say when confronted, and took responsibility for people's feelings, especially the feelings that she was being blamed for.

Below is a list of the some of the self-beliefs that I planted in my subconscious mind from my encounter with Mrs. Albertelli. As you read through these ask yourself, what would I grow from these seeds if they were planted in my mind? Then take a minute and review a moment or a lifetime of interactions with one of your antagonists. What seeds did you plant from your interactions with them and how did those seeds grow into some of your struggles?

- *I can't trust my words.*
- *I can't trust my friends.*
- *I create danger with my words.*
- *It is not safe to say what I want, because someone will show up and use my words against me.*
- *My words cause attack.*
- *I never say the right thing.*
- *I deserve to be punished for what I say.*
- *I don't deserve friends.*
- *My words hurt people.*
- *The words that I say make me unlikeable.*
- *I am not likable.*
- *I am a disgrace.*

- *I disappoint myself with my words.*
- *I disappoint my family with my words.*
- *I disappoint my friends with my words.*
- *I am embarrassment.*
- *My words create embarrassment.*
- *When I say what I want to say I humiliate myself.*
- *I am humiliation.*
- *I am 100% responsible for everyone's feelings, so no matter what I say or don't say, it is my fault.*
- *Others use me to perpetuate their own inner drama.*
- *I am singled out for being me.*
- *I am not free to be me.*
- *I am to blame for everything.*
- *It is always my fault.*

The self-beliefs that grew within the deep soil of my subconscious mind from these two life experiences were incongruent with the love that is my true nature (and your true nature too). My antagonist's words and actions, through my own self-perceptions, covertly programmed my human operating system with behaviors and emotional outputs that produced my suffering, my insecurities, and the relationships that preyed on my disempowerment.

As a result, I built my closest relationships with people who embodied more confidence and more creativity than I believed I possessed. I surrounded myself with people who I perceived were smarter and more trustworthy than myself. Because I subconsciously didn't believe I was smart enough, I dated boys and married a man who I thought were all smarter and more capable than me. The men I attracted were usually controlling, because it was always safer to put the decision making into their hands, so I was released from the responsibility of getting it wrong. Though I've had good friends in my life, that list also includes "friends" who have publicly and privately humiliated and attacked me.

My subconscious self-beliefs were the patterns that repeated themselves in my relationships. They told the story of how I'd outsourced my power to people I thought possessed the qualities I believed I was lacking. Knowing that my past was creating my present made deconstructing the experiences that contributed to my not-love subconscious self-beliefs all the more important. If I wanted a different present, I needed to weed out of my subconscious mind the self-beliefs that had grown deep roots from the seeds of my not-love life experiences.

We make sense of and process what has happened to us through language. In my experience, our thoughts mostly communicate to us in word and sentence form, just like how we communicate with others. Even if you see a picture in your mind, to make sense of that image you put language to it. What I've learned from my personal experience with the subconscious mind is that your self-beliefs get stored as the sentences from your unaware thoughts that then act as the *code* that operates your conscious self; the you that develops from the seeds you planted in your subconscious mind.

When you release these sentences that communicate your self-beliefs from your subconscious mind, they no longer influence the thoughts, feelings, emotions, and behaviors that consciously come through you. A few more examples of subconscious programs (sentences) I've identified in my own subconscious mind and then released are below.

- *I have to prove to everyone that I am enough.*
- *I have to convince people that I am lovable.*
- *I am responsible for everyone's emotions.*
- *I am a disappointment.*
- *What I have to say doesn't matter.*
- *As a woman, it is not safe to be seen/heard.*
- *As a woman, it is my job to serve.*
- *My feelings/needs don't matter.*
- *To be worthy of love I must sacrifice my needs for others.*
- *As a woman, I must sacrifice my needs for others (especially men).*
- *My needs don't matter.*

Becoming consciously aware of your subconscious mind is important, because it's your subconscious self-beliefs that feed your inner discontent. They provoke your addictions and your depression. They cause you to hurt yourself and others. They ignite your judgments. They incite drama in your relationships and disease in your body. They motivate you to write unkind words and then post them on social media. They embolden you to say hurtful things or nothing at all, because you are too afraid to stand up for yourself. They convince you to lie. They make you a bully, or a wallflower, or a people pleaser, or a narcissist. They rob you of your happiness, self-love, and feelings of peace. On a larger scale, they start wars to kill people for money and resources. They unplug you and all of us from our true, powered-with-love, selves.

If you feel disharmony in your life, your mind is still working perfectly; however, your mind is sending information that is out of tune with your ability to empower love (of self and others) and create peace in your life. Any form of dissonance or discord is your soul trying to get your attention to wake up and pay attention because there is something that needs to be healed. My unhappy feelings, my fears, and my physical body were sending me loads of information, begging me, through my struggles and my suffering, to wake up and discover the root causes. Awakening to the information that I'd unknowingly hidden away in the warehouse of my subconscious mind profoundly changed my life.

Start listening to what you are saying. Journal about your thoughts, your experiences, and your feelings. Your subconscious mind is operating your conscious self, so as you talk or write, your subconscious thoughts will make themselves known. You've got to be tuned-in through self-awareness to start listening for them. *Love Ignites Peace: Our Next Evolu-*

tion, The Companion Journal takes you on a guided process to help you start identifying and releasing those not-love beliefs, so that you can embody the peace and the freedom that comes with truly and unconditionally loving yourself and others.

I loved myself, just enough, to have the courage to start unpacking my suitcase of not-love self-beliefs. Did I really want to go revisit all of my painful memories and dig up the shame and humiliation that I'd felt? No, not really; but I knew that understanding the subconscious self-beliefs that I'd created from those moments would allow me to transform my life into a different set of experiences. Sometimes I would take myself out of the experience and imagine two characters in a play acting out the experience that had hurt me.

When I disconnected from the experience and looked at it as *information,* it disempowered my emotional charge. It was through the process of facing my most challenging relationships, memories, and traumas that I was able to find out who I'd become as a result of their influence. With that knowing, I was empowered to empty the mental trash of their toxic effects, and to become the love that I'd been seeking.

I'd long ago let go of that kindergarten moment, but I ventured back to that experience because I knew this event held important information about myself. It took me many years to let go of my interaction with Mrs. Albertelli, but eventually through the subconscious work and using *Love's 6 Actions,* I was able to forgive both myself and her. What

I'd actually written into my subconscious mind from my interaction with these two adults remained anonymous to my conscious awareness until I decided to put my waders on and walk heart-deep through the muck of my disempowered unhappiness.

What are the experiences you remember from your childhood? Your memories are important because there is valuable information within them connected to your subconscious mind.

If you remember what seems like an inconsequential moment from your childhood, write it down. There is a reason that you remember, usually connected to the intensity of the emotional response that you felt. The reason that kindergarten memory stayed with me was because my emotional response was so intense that even decades later, I couldn't forget. Same with the Suzanne Albertelli moment.

Your emotional response turns up the volume on any moment when you are experiencing the extremes associated with the fantastic or the horrible. They are the energy, like fire, that burns the meanings your subconscious creates about yourself into your mind. The more intense your energy feels about an experience, the louder that moment becomes in your mind.

As your mind is interpreting yourself amongst all of the external information, your emotional response is putting exclamation marks around the extreme moments and periods next to the mundane/normal moments. Your not-love emotions are telling you something isn't right, and it is in learning to listen to those emotions, past and present, that the information in your subconscious mind can be discovered.

Paying attention to your emotions and your long-term feelings is another important source of self-information. Your secret subconscious self-beliefs are the birthplace from where your not-love feelings and emotions arise. They are the information that gives life to your emotional response and the residue of your long-term feelings. Like a trail of breadcrumbs, your feelings and emotions can lead you back to their source—your hidden subconscious self-beliefs.

If you experience any of the following feelings and emotions that suck the joy out of you, backtracking through your life's memories can help you identify some of the self-meanings that have contributed to those feelings. Additionally, becoming self-aware in the present moment when you are flooded with a not-love emotion gives you an immediate interaction to start analyzing.

unhappy	sorrowful	wounded
melancholic	down	heartbroken
despondent	depressed	angry
resentful	bitter	furious
enraged	irritated	annoyed
frustrated	outraged	lonely
isolated	abandoned	rejected
unwanted	unseen	misunderstood
afraid	anxious	fearful

insecure	worried	panicked
unsettled	uneasy	nervous
apprehensive	ashamed	guilty
regretful	remorseful	embarrassed
humiliated	self-blaming	hopeless
helpless	powerless	disempowered
defeated	discouraged	depleted
drained	overwhelmed	conflicted
torn	confused	uncertain
lost	directionless	jealous
envious	threatened	betrayed

What was said that made you feel so angry, frustrated, annoyed or irritated? Then, without blaming the other person, ask *why* their words ignited your emotional response.

Becoming acutely aware of your emotions and your long-term feelings leads you back to the subconscious self-beliefs that cause your emotions and feelings. I would feel so hurt and angry when my husband criticized me. His words pulled the trigger on my emotional response, but my subconscious self-beliefs had already loaded our interaction with the gunpowder required for my reaction. My subconscious beliefs were the ignition source that lit the fuse to my anger and other not-love emotions.

Because my subconscious mind believed I wasn't enough, that I was responsible for his feelings, and that I was a disappointment, his critical words set my anger ablaze. *The cause of my anger was my subconscious beliefs, not his words.*

My emotional reaction was the effect. The anger I felt was me unknowingly fighting against the subconscious beliefs I didn't want to be true. When your subconscious mind carries beliefs that are out of alignment with your true nature–love, your emotional response rises up and resists with all of its might. They instigate the explosive emotions you experience, and they become the long-term feelings that cause you to feel depressed, anxious or unhappy.

In retrospect, his words might not have even been critical of me, but my subconscious self-beliefs immediately caused me to interpret them as such. It took practice to stop blaming him and to start becoming self-aware enough to start listening for the *information* behind my emotions and my long-term feelings.

I used to believe it was my story's antagonists that were causing the dull ache of my unhappiness, but they were only contributors to the not-love self-beliefs that I'd unknowingly written about myself. Though they created a challenging not-love experience for me, it was ultimately my mind that interpreted myself from their actions. Instead of feeling victimized by blame, I decided to take responsibility for the self-beliefs I'd created from the interaction. I made a choice to get rid of what was provoking my anger and feeding my long-term feelings of unhappiness and disempowerment, so I could create a different experience for myself and for others.

When someone's words or actions toward you ignite your anger, your emotions are giving you a signal that there is a subconscious belief that is out of alignment. If your self-beliefs say you are 100% loved and loveable, that you matter and that life supports you in all of its unlimited goodness, then you won't be provoked by other people's words and actions. Your feelings will be reflecting happiness, self-trust and confidence, because your self-beliefs align with those feelings. What's more, you will have the self-awareness to accept others and allow them to have their own experience, because you understand it is their subconscious self-beliefs that are feeding their feelings and emotions. You will be peace in action.

Thanks to my improved health, receiving the words *Love Ignites Peace,* and the woman who taught me about my subconscious mind, so began my self-awareness road trip to a new destination full of unconditionally loving myself and others. This wasn't a process of judging myself or putting my life into boxes of right or wrong. It was a heartfelt unraveling of looking at my life through the lens of what I'd experienced, and then how I'd interpreted myself from those experiences. How had other people's pain become my limitations?

You should never label what you discover
about yourself as bad or wrong. Your not-love
subconscious programs are just information about
how your mind unknowingly interpreted yourself
within the totality of your life's experiences.
Becoming aware of what those beliefs are is your

unique journey back to self-awareness. Then you can consciously reunite with the love that is your authentic, potential-filled, human self.

Changing my subconscious mind and silencing the not-love voices that were keeping me limited and trapped in unhappiness took time, patience, willingness, vulnerability, curiosity, and courage. It had taken me 40 plus years to secure all of the self-beliefs that I'd adopted from my relationships, others' expectations of me, not-love suggestions about me, culture, and my religious programming. There was no quick fix.

It was one of the biggest and most transformative exercises of my lifetime, as I patiently brought my not-love subconscious self-beliefs into my conscious mind, and then released them using the subconscious technique that I'd been taught. Anyone can release their own subconscious programs and help others release theirs, it just requires a little bit of training.

I will always be the main character, the hero, in my story, just like you are the hero in your story. I made a choice that I no longer wanted my subconscious mind to play the self-destructive role it had previously created in my life. You too are empowered to make that choice when and if the time is right for you.

What I've discovered over the years with the subconscious mind is that although we've all had unique life experiences, many of our subconscious programs are very similar. When the not-love belief is released, the positive, love-in-action belief automatically installs itself; because the positive is part of the truth (love) of who we are as human beings. In order to evolve beyond suffering and struggles, we have to awaken to what is in our subconscious minds that is keeping us from creating experiences for ourselves and others that empower love, peace, abundance, and joy.

It is your subconscious mind that determines your very personal relationship with love.

ASSIMILATING CHAPTER 5:

Do you see yourself in any of the subconscious programs that I list? Which ones? How have they manifested as your feelings, emotions and behaviors? What relationship patterns have they attracted into your life? How are these programs connected to your most challenging relationships?

_____

_____

_____

_____

_____

_____

_____

_____

_____

_____

_____

_____

_____

_____

_____

_____

_____

_____

_____

_____

_____

_____

_____

_____

_____

_____

_____

_____

_____

_____

_____

_____

Our Next Evolution

_____

_____

_____

_____

_____

_____

_____

_____

_____

_____

_____

_____

_____

_____

_____

_____

_____

_____

_____

_____

_____

_____

6
The Duality Challenge

QUESTIONS FOR CONTEMPLATION
AS YOU DIGEST CHAPTER 6:

How do you interact with duality? Which of duality's
3 aspects motivates and/or challenges you the most?

Duality, the state of having two different parts, adds huge elements of complexity and creates unlimited combinations of experiences for us to learn from. It affects our experiences and it directly affects what we unknowingly stash in our subconscious human operating system. We live in a dual environment. Every day when the sun rises, we have light, and then the sun sets and we have darkness—the outer edges of the same spectrum of energy, light and dark.

Experiencing a range of opposing energies is part of our human experience. Duality is a paradox because it creates experience from contradictory energies. Positive and negative, love and fear, war and peace, separation and unity, judgment and discernment, good and bad, right and wrong, are a few examples of dual energies. Everything on this planet has an opposite energy. It is up to each of us to become aware of this and choose how we use duality to create our experiences.

Duality may be one of our greatest challenges to overcome as we evolve our consciousness from the old to the new—*Love Ignites Peace*. Operating from duality's not-love in action energies has made our personal limitations and our collective suffering profound. When we are treated from duality's not-love end of the spectrum, we interpret ourselves from those not-love words and actions. We believe we are bad, a disappointment, undeserving, or that life is a dangerous experience that needs to be feared. Our once joyful inner child becomes afraid and wounded. Then we take our hurt out into the world and try and create our lives from the not-love side of duality. What happens? We program our minds with not-love subconscious self-beliefs, which influence the behaviors that perpetuate our individual and collective suffering.

Becoming aware that our lives are a set of experiences that we are here to learn from was one of my big self-awareness breakthroughs. Understanding duality's polarizing effect on the not-love subconscious beliefs that I'd created about myself, and how the collective has suffered at the misuse of duality's energies, made me see our human experience through the perspective of a game. Once I had this insight, I knew I had a choice to make. How did I want to interact with duality? Duality is part of how we've learned to interact with ourselves and each other. Again we can't change what we aren't aware of.

Duality itself creates an infinite range of emotions and thought/belief combinations. It has greatly challenged us in the past because we weren't aware of how we were using duality to create our individual and collective consciousness. The experiences that we've created for each other have been filled with suffering, because we lacked the self-awareness to understand the pain created by the not-love effects of duality in our own lives. Our hurts, our lack, and our limitations were installed in our subconscious minds as we interacted with others, and then created meanings (self-beliefs) about ourselves from their words, actions, and nonverbal cues. Our self-beliefs then directly influenced how we treated our friends, our family, our co-workers, and even the strangers that crossed our path.

Love has been here with us and has created beautiful experiences in our individual lives, but even that love has been twisted within each of us by not-love experiences. We respond with love's helping hands during a natural disaster, and then return to not-love rhetoric when confronted with beliefs that oppose our own. Duality has separated us from our authentic, innately loving selves, and our connection as a collective human community.

If you were surrounded by negativity, then you learned how to filter life through the negative end of duality (negative vs positive). If you were surrounded by kindness, then you learned to treat others from the kindness end of duality (meanness vs kindness). If you were brought up in a house where conflict and drama ruled, then you learned how to get attention and solve problems from the conflict end of duality (conflict vs harmony). Your beliefs chose you, because you weren't yet aware you had a choice to create different self-beliefs, and you had no idea of the experience your soul chose before you were born.

The majority of our self-beliefs are anchored into our subconscious minds in childhood. Additionally, you had no idea that the people you were interacting with were behaving within the spectrum of duality. You were just a child taking in the wonder of the world and interpreting yourself from your environment and your important relationships. The not-love energies on duality's spectrum created more not-love beliefs, and love's beliefs held you steady as you negotiated life.

Duality interacts with your experiences in three different ways.

1) Sometimes you need to *choose the outer edges of duality* to create a loving experience.
2) Other times you need to *balance a dual energy.*
3) Duality's darker energies often *create experiences that motivate* you to make big life changes for the better.

We have been oblivious to the reality that when we judge someone as "bad," it is the energy of duality at work. If we label a person "good" or if we stay neutral, then an entirely different energy is created in that situation, that person and ourselves.

Our self-beliefs greatly influence how we choose to interact with duality, just like duality influences our self-beliefs. Looking at your life through the lens of *What have I learned about myself from my life's experiences?* can illuminate how duality has affected who you have become. Duality can be a tool that creates infinite combinations of experiences for you. Expanding your self-awareness includes recognizing where you land on duality's spectrum as part of your own human consciousness.

Positive and negative are another example of dual energies. They are the same energy, just opposite ends of one very long range. Victim and co-creator are also expressions of the same energy. Like positive and negative, how we interact with the victim and co-creator energies creates vastly different experiences. Duality invites us to the *outer edges* of its energy to create, so it is up to us to decide which end we choose. Positivity energizes life and vitalizes harmony; it is one of love as an action's descriptive words. Negativity focuses on lack and limitations. Feeling and acting as a victim depletes our happiness, makes us feel helpless, and paralyzes our ability to see beyond our pain.

Acting as an empowered co-creator allows us to thrive and play within life's unlimited potential. Living our lives from the opposite of love in action (not-love) has disconnected us from our true-selves, which live on the *Love's 6 Actions* side of duality.

Separation from love's all-things-good energies has created pain and suffering, while unifying with love supports the heart-opening freedoms of unlimited self-expression. Separation and unity are dual energies themselves. The more we live unified with love's all-things-good energies, the more we are able to allow others to authentically express themselves without judgment or verbal persecution; we become more enlightened in how we interact with duality. One key to overcoming the duality paradox in our human experience is to always choose the positive energies that promote love as an action.

Interacting with the qualities on the right side of the list below promotes love's all-things-good energy.

Victim . . . . . . Co-Creator

Scarcity . . . . . . Abundance

Separation . . . . . . Unity

Differences . . . . . . Commonalities

Judgment . . . . . . Discernment

Disappointment . . . . . . Encouragement

Drama . . . . . . Peace

Shame . . . . . . Respect

Danger . . . . . . Safety

Fear . . . . . . Love

Fear and love have been one of our greatest duality challenges. Fear has ruled and love has taken a backseat to the experience that we've all created for each other. It could be said that any energy which doesn't promote love is an action fueled by fear. For example, why do we judge someone, shame someone, or create drama? Because there is something lacking in ourselves, a fear that we aren't safe, or a valuable, important, significant human being. Just like little kids, we act out to cover up our deepest fear, that we aren't loveable. We seek attention, even if it is negative, to try and fill this inner void.

For much of the world our basic needs are met, yet we still fear for our survival. The news is designed to report the bad, and every other advertisement is about a drug we need because we are sick. When did being sick instead of healthy become the norm? Healthy and sick are another example of duality. Fear creeps into our minds from feeling unsafe or not having enough to survive. Disease creeps into our minds creating beliefs that focus on our sickness verses our health. Death scares us, because we fear the unknown or the end of our consciousness. We fear suffering, yet our suffering is being perpetuated by more fear.

Fear's roots have grown deep within each of us and our collective human community. If we could change one way that we deal with duality, let's end fear's sovereign reign and choose to rule our lives with love's end of that dual energy. *Fear Ignites Suffering* is the dual energy of *Love Ignites Peace.*

Another duality challenge is that some dual energies need to be *balanced*, instead of picking a side. The need to be right (right and wrong) is a dual energy that needs to be balanced, because that energy can polarize (divide). If you feel the need to push your rightness and someone else's wrong-ness, you land on the outer edges of that energy which has a greater potential to create disharmony. When we become more neutral and less emboldened to stand in our rightness, we create more harmonizing interactions.

The reason for your need to be right is contained within the self-beliefs that you unknowingly constructed from your life experiences. As humans we seek to be validated and want to believe we are significant. It is because of dual-ity's not-love energies that you don't already believe you are important and valuable. A person that already feels signifi-cant has no need to be self-righteous. We focus on our dif-ferences instead of our commonalities to make us feel more important.

Wrong — Wisdom (Balance)— Right

Dual energies that need to be balanced divide us if we aren't aware of them. Democrat and Republican are dual energies that keep us divided. How many people have told you that they are in the middle and really not one or the other (bal-ance)? It is a system set up, which polarizes, because we are only given two choices.

Masculine and feminine are an example of dual ener-gies, seeking balance. When these energies are out of bal-ance, the division affects how we interact with ourselves and our collective human community. Our societies have been constructed with overwhelmingly masculine principles, while the feminine principles needed to create collaboration, peace, and good for the collective have been largely ignored. If we act too masculine, we are so competition and action focused that we force and control instead of allow, collaborate, and flow, which is the feminine expression. This example can be turned around. It might be that we only flow and allow, never taking action to make a change or to protect ourselves. The gender each individual chooses doesn't matter, because regardless of how we identify, we all express along the spectrum of masculine and feminine energies. Like the divided sides of our brain, masculine and feminine energy seek unity; a balance that comes from using the wisdom found in the best aspects of both qualities equally.

Science and common sense, greed and generosity, work and rest, and boundaries or lack thereof are other examples of dual energies that require balance. Science not balanced by common sense can create situations that promote ideas or products that appear to be technologically advanced, but aren't good for the planet or our collective human community. This can be seen with foods that contain chemicals and genetic modifications. The science was discovered to apply these formulations into our food supply, but the common sense that human health would suffer when they are consumed was lacking.

We are programmed with the belief that profits at all costs rule. Making a profit is a good thing, and when everyone enjoys the abundance of living a profitable life or running a profitable company, then everyone benefits; but profit, when it turns to greed, can create suffering for individuals and our collective human community. On the other side sits extreme generosity. When you are generous to a fault, you give so much away that there is nothing left for you to enjoy your life.

Work that is not balanced with rest, both mental and physical, disrupts our health and our ability to enjoy life. If we only rest, we are robbed of the work that can add purpose to our lives. A life without boundaries keeps us too open, and a life with too many boundaries keeps us too closed. Either end, without balance, has the potential to create experiences that enrich our pain and bankrupt our happiness. Love as an action supplies the wisdom to balance dual energies so healthy relationships and decisions based in the highest good can evolve.

Wisdom is the pivot point within your consciousness that empowers love in action. It creates balance by combining your knowledge, experiences, and your self-awareness with the actions that promote the all-things-good energies of love. Dual energies that require balance have strengths connected with the outer edges of their nature, but too much of one energy, without the counterbalance of the strengths of the opposing energy, deprives you of the wholeness and the empowerment to build a happy and peaceful life—the wisdom found in the balanced expression.

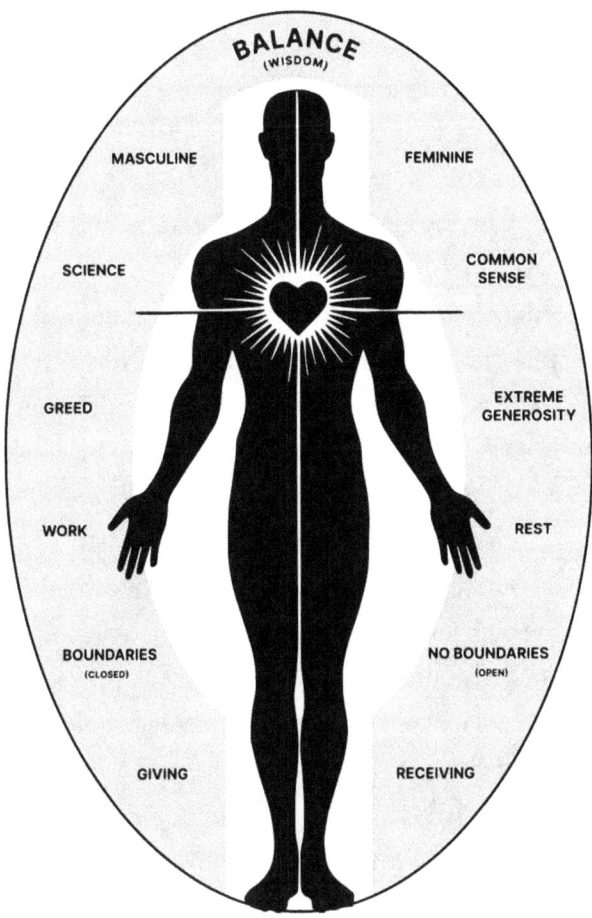

Giving and receiving, dual energies that also require balance, are important for us to explore. They are energies that greatly influence how, when the gifts from both energies are fully expressed and balanced, the prolific garden of love's goodness can be enjoyed. As humans we love to give. We give generously of our time, our money, our talents, and gifts for special occasions and ordinary moments. Though some people have trouble giving, we are primarily taught to give through society and our religious training.

Receiving is rarely mentioned as an important part of our human experience. In order for the gifts contained in both sides of giving and receiving to be fully embraced, their dual energies need to be balanced. If you aren't fully open to receiving then you've created resistance in your ability receive the wholeness of life's infinite goodness. Giving too much can deplete you mentally, emotionally, and even physically.

Exploring and then releasing the not-love self-beliefs, which I'd installed in my subconscious human operating system about my inability to receive, empowered me to receive my own goodness (love), and enabled me to create in partnership with life, versus in resistance to life's goodness. Life itself is a partner that is always putting people, information, and synchronicities in your path to help you achieve your human potential.

Through these gifts, love in action is constantly giving to you and trying to support your heart's greatest desires. If you aren't open to receiving, then your ability to accept that goodness is obstructed. For example, if you've blocked your ability to receive abundance, then how will you create abundance? Opportunities for abundance are everywhere, but unavailable to you if you can't receive them. Or if you can't receive love, how can you love yourself and others? There are many people who want to love you, but if you can't receive their love, they can't give you the love that you are seeking.

As you explore your relationship with receiving, ask yourself, "Can I receive my worthiness, my enoughness, the knowing that I matter, that I am significant, and that I am loveable?" Then ask, "Am I open to receiving the all-things-good energies of love like joy, happiness, abundance, great health, and peace?" Examining your ability to receive could be some of the most important self-awareness work that you do, because when you are open to receiving all of the good that life has to offer, you empower your co-creative abilities to work in harmony with life's infinite possibilities—you ignite your human potential which is love in action.

As I asked why my ability to receive had been closed down, the subconscious seeds which I'd unknowingly planted from the self-meanings I'd created from my experiences started rising to my conscious mind. As I dug deeper into my self-beliefs, I discovered that I'd shut down my ability to receive because my self-beliefs told me people would love me more if I played small, instead of allowing my brilliant, authentic light to shine.

My relationship with receiving was further complicated by the self-beliefs I'd unknowingly installed from my junior high trauma. When I was being shouted at and told how bad I was for saying something so awful, I shut down my ability to receive or hear what was being said about me; it was just too painful for me to absorb the words. From that moment on until I became self-aware, any form of conflict would cause me to go deaf. Mentally and emotionally, I would leave the conversation; I couldn't accept all of the pain that my imperfections had caused, because the harsh words reinforced the belief I wasn't good enough. Within trauma's fallout, my ability to receive the good was also compromised.

Unraveling your relationship with giving is just as important. Not being able to give signifies feelings of lack and limitation. Are you afraid that you won't have enough for yourself if you give to others? Do you give with strings attached so you manipulate what you receive in return? Or are you afraid that what you have to give, whether it is time, your talents, or a physical gift, isn't good enough?

Emotions and their responses also require balance. When we live in an unbalanced state of either blocking our emotions or emotionally spiraling, we are creating an unhealthy and unbalanced experience for ourselves. When a person shuts down their ability to process their emotions, it creates an inner dam, clogged with anger's volatility and frustration's defeat, a quagmire of feelings waiting to explode and create more not-love with whoever is in the way. Spiraling emotions are equally as unhealthy. When we spiral for days and even years on an emotion created from one of our not-love experiences, we feed our victimhood and become depressed, anxious, and even sick. Emotions are meant to be felt, processed, and then released.

When a not-love emotion overtakes me, I allow myself

to feel what I am experiencing and then I dig deeper; for me this is the processing. Instead of feeling victimized by what happened, I ask, "What is the self-belief that triggered this feeling?" When the self-belief arises from my subconscious mind to my conscious mind, I am empowered to release the belief and the emotional response that it caused. *The Companion Journal* to this book takes you through a lifetime of exercises that help you explore your emotions and their provoking self-beliefs. Our not-love emotions are the shout-outs to our self-awareness. Pay attention because they are telling you that something is out of balance.

Creating experiences from of the outer edges of dual energies that require balance causes individual and collective suffering. The ranges of dual energies that need to be balanced contain lifetimes of self-beliefs that must be disentangled so that love in action can express as peace. If your actions express as more masculine than feminine, balance doesn't mean you deny the qualities of your masculine expression. It means you bring your feminine energy up to meet your masculine energy (or vice versa) and create balance from the best characteristics of those energies.

The same with giving and receiving. If you are better at giving, explore what is blocking your ability to receive. Then, bring your ability to receive up to meet your ability to give, and create balance from both the joy of giving and the joy of receiving. Evaluating how you are expressing dual energies and the self-beliefs that influence your behaviors creates an opportunity to assert the best of both, which will help you achieve mental and emotional balance. Dual energies that require balance must be brought into equilibrium in order for you to become love and live your human potential.

If our thoughts/self-beliefs create our reality, then understanding how experiences are created within duality's energy spectrum empowers us to choose how we want to create our actions. Choose the outer edges of dual energies that align with love in action and balance the energies that require love in action.

> *When you become aware of the duality paradox,*
> *you have the information you need to*
> *make a wise choice, both in how you*
> *interact and how you respond.*

My relationship with my husband taught me how duality interacts with *Love's 6 Actions*. That relationship challenged my courage to take action by helping me to balance my masculine side with my feminine side. I had to take control of my feelings and of my personal experience, and then take action to make a change. It helped me understand how the pain, suffering, and trauma from our stories, the not-love ends of duality's energies, kept us perpetuating those destructive behavior patterns with each other. The knowledge that hurt people hurt other people empowered my discernment and moved me past judgment.

The last part of duality's paradox is that *our inner dis-*

content can be the catalyst which fuels our biggest leaps in self-growth. The irony found in our not-love feelings is that they have the power to motivate us to evolve into the love we want to become. Are you tired of fighting with your mom or being steamrolled by that co-worker? Are you afraid to quit your job and do what you've always been called to do? Are you fed up with the dysfunctional partners that you seem to always attract? It was my inner angst that ignited my desire to return to my light. My health problems and my disempowered unhappiness were duality's dark side that pushed me to start making changes in my life. *Love Ignites Peace* was the love as an action end of duality that motivated me to understand myself from my past experiences. Previously, beliefs that kept me limited and afraid had ignited my suffering. Now love encouraged me to shift my consciousness and let all of that go. It was time to love myself, physically, mentally, emotionally, and spiritually—the whole of me. Understanding duality makes living *Love Ignites Peace* easier, because it puts awareness into how you choose to respond.

Our current problems, filled with suffering and conflict, have been caused by individuals choosing to live at the not-love ends and the imbalanced expressions of duality's energies. Exploring your relationship with duality's various energies can bring self-awareness to the seeds of belief that unknowingly blossomed into the life you created. You empower your ability to become love in action when you start exploring your relationship with duality.

As you deconstruct yourself and become aware of how duality has affected your life's experiences and influenced your subconscious mind, then you can shift your behaviors from perpetuating separation to cultivating unity. *Love Ignites Peace* asks us to see duality for what it is, a tool that creates infinite *experiences* for us to learn from. With this awareness, we can choose to transcend any and all energies that create suffering, divisiveness, and separation. *Love Ignites Peace*, as a new consciousness to solve our old problems, challenges us to ascend beyond duality's trappings to create peace. Just as love creates peace, learning how to overcome duality's many paradoxes also creates the experience of peace.

Duality is a tool that creates unlimited experiences for us to learn from and then evolve beyond to a different experience. Duality has the power to act as a catalyst for our personal and planetary evolution.

Are we ready to evolve beyond living in duality from not-love and transform our personal consciousness (self-awareness) to love in action's side of duality? When we make that huge leap in awareness we will create a different experience for ourselves, individually and for the human collective. *Love's 6 Actions* will guide us to peace.

Three Ways Duality Interacts With Love

1) **Choice**—Choose the outer positive edge of duality that promotes love in action.
2) **Balance**—Balance love in action.
3) **Inner discontent**—motivates transformation to love.

DEFINITIONS

Duality

The contrast between two aspects of opposing energies that through their interaction create experiences from their contradictory natures.

Wisdom

A quality that seeks the highest good in all situations. It is obtained through your knowledge and the self-awareness that you bring to your life's experiences. It is the response that promotes love of self and love of others.

ASSIMILATING CHAPTER 6:

*How do you interact with duality? Which of duality's
3 aspects motivates and/or challenges you the most?*

_____

_____

_____

_____

_____

_____

_____

_____

_____

_____

_____

_____

_____

_____

_____

_____

_____

_____

_____

Our Next Evolution

_____

_____

_____

_____

_____

_____

_____

_____

_____

_____

_____

_____

_____

_____

_____

_____

_____

_____

_____

_____

_____

_____

Our Next Evolution

7

Love's 6 Actions—Love of Self

CHALLENGE: Identify your own experiences within each of Love's 6 Actions – Love of Self.

Understand Your Story

Understanding your story may be the most important action of *Love's 6 Actions*. When you take the time to deeply understand your story, you are taking the time to become acutely self-aware. From your life's experiences, which include your impactful relationships, your memorable moments, and your traumas, you subconsciously installed your self-love and not-love self-beliefs into your human operating system. You became your story, whether you realized it or not. It is from your story that you learned how to be the person you are.

You became what you observed by perceiving yourself within your environment. From the time you were a newborn and even now, you perceive and interpret who you believe yourself to be from your surroundings and the relationships that fill up your life. The ecosystem of your life's conditions provides the information for your mind to tell you who you think you are. All of those self-perceptions turned into your self-beliefs, which have influenced your feelings, your behaviors, and what you've attracted into your life. When you feel triggered by someone or some event, it is because a not-love self-belief is lying under the surface.

Understanding your story is not an exercise in blame, nor is the process engineered for you to hang on to your past. Just the opposite, it is a process of standing in your vulnerability so you can deeply understand yourself and discover the limiting self-beliefs that you unknowingly picked up along the way; the information from your experiences that hold you back from completely (100%) loving yourself.

Taking the time to deeply understand your story is not living in the past, but looking at the past's influences (information) so that you can transcend the limitations that have prevented you from unconditionally loving yourself and others. You can't evolve beyond what you aren't aware of.

Understanding your story aligns you with all of the things you already love about yourself, and it reveals the baggage that keeps you from fully loving yourself. Understanding your story is a process of asking yourself, "What meanings or self-interpretations did I make about myself from my relationships, my traumas, and the environment I was raised in?"

As you understand those meanings, you are connecting with your subconscious mind, the part of your mind that acts as your human operating system. The meanings that you, without awareness, make up about yourself as you perceive yourself within your relationships and your environment, get installed as the *code* that determines your ability to love yourself in all situations. The suggestions people make about you to you also get added to your subconscious self-beliefs.

If you were told that you'd never be a success, or that you were fat and ugly, or that you were creative and talented, your young mind (and even your adult mind) accepts those suggestions and then stores them in the basement of your subconscious mind. They get added to a list of beliefs you unknowingly carry with you, which can make loving and accepting yourself a challenge. Those beliefs affect how you feel and how you interact with yourself and others. Your negative subconscious self-beliefs are the gunpowder that ignite your triggers, the hot coals that keep your emotions burning for days and even years, and the smoke signal that works like the law of attraction.

What you believe about yourself directly influences who and what you attract into your life. If you believe you aren't good enough, then you will attract people into your life that treat you as such. Or if you believe life is dangerous and unstable, you will attract people and circumstances that demonstrate this belief to you.

When you say you "can't," there is a self-belief stashed in your subconscious mind telling you, for a number of possible reasons, why you can't. For me a big "can't" was that I am not smart enough. Self-doubt, self-distrust, and fear for my safety, unknowingly installed in my subconscious mind during my childhood, all contributed to the many times in my life where "can't" determined my decisions and my behaviors. Your reasons are personal to you. Ask yourself, "Why can't I?"

Fear operates the same way. Self-beliefs fueled by fear's side of duality prevent you from following your heart's desires. Fear keeps you sequestered in limitation and lack. It feeds your anxiety and even your depression. Your past affects both your present and the decisions you make that affect your future. My greatest fear was that I wasn't capable of taking care of myself, therefore I made sure I surrounded myself with people who I perceived were more capable than me, even if those people weren't good for me. What are you afraid of? Fear is the opposite of love, and fear keeps you from fully loving yourself.

A friend recently related the story to me that the only way she could get attention from her mom was when she pretended to be sick. She remembers as a toddler intentionally coughing in her crib so her mom would come and get her. Crying didn't make her mom pay attention to her, but being sick did. As she looked at her life through the lens of her story and the meanings she created about herself, she was surprised to discover that her self-interpretation from this experience made her believe that the only way to get attention was to be sick. In her young mind, she perceived that her mom cared about her when she was sick, so she became sick in order to feel loved. This wasn't a conscious behavior, but one that she installed as a child in her subconscious mind, her human operating system.

She was a child wounded by the self-belief that her mom didn't care enough to pay attention to her needs. Unbeknownst to her, she created self-beliefs that told her she would be loved if she was sick. Translate that subconscious belief into her day-to-day adult life, and she was always sick or having an accident. She wasn't even aware that this was happening, but as she dissected her story into bite sized memories and looked at how she perceived herself from the early interactions with her mom, she gained greater self-awareness and made an important self-discovery.

As an adult she unknowingly continued the pattern of using sickness as a way to get attention and to feel loved, not just from her mom but from others too. Somewhere along the way her mind, without awareness, told her she wasn't important or loveable when she was healthy. When she made this self-discovery, she was empowered with the knowledge she needed to change that belief. Once she was aware, she could transform beyond this limiting belief. Taking the time to deeply understand her story gave her the insight she needed to start healing and loving that wounded part of herself.

Different situations happen for each of us within duality's infinite combination of experiences, but most of us carry some kind of mental and emotional scarring. Using sickness is just one way of seeking the attention that eludes us. If there is any part of you that doesn't feel valued, significant, or that you are an important human being who matters, then there is a not-love self-belief that is connected to your story.

Building love of self will help you know with conviction that you matter. Figure out why you don't think you matter, let go of blame of self and others, and do the work to overcome this limitation. It will free you to spread your wings and soar on joy's weightless currents. When you start to identify your limiting self-beliefs, you expand your self-awareness so you can overcome what is keeping you from loving yourself.

After my gluten intolerance diagnosis, the fog that had disconnected me from myself lifted. An inner light that was barely flickering ignited. With newfound clarity, I knew that I needed to understand how I had ended up feeling so lost and unhappy. A strong knowing, that I didn't realize at the time was my intuition, guided me to my story. There had to be reasons from my past that had contributed to the decisions that had created my future. As a young girl I felt so filled up with joy, but somewhere along the way joy moved out and unhappiness remodeled the me that I once knew.

I started journaling, pouring out my feelings and having conversations with the young me. First, I decided to focus on all of the good in my life, past and present. Gratitude for all of the wonderful parts of my life poured out of my pen into my heart. From my happy memories and my encouraging relationships, I could see an inner structure that held enough self-love to support me as I started my self-discovery expedition. It was my intention to reinforce that foundation and then deconstruct what my not-love self-beliefs had created. The blueprint for the *me* that I wanted to build arrived when I received the words *Love Ignites Peace*.

Fortified from my loving memories, I shed my protective armor and stepped naked into my vulnerability. What had happened to me? If I remembered an incident, no matter how small or trivial I thought it was, I wrote it down. I remembered camping with my grandparents, which I always loved to do, and deciding to tell the jokes I'd heard at school. My grandma didn't think they were funny; dirty, she called them. The next day she told my parents that I was telling dirty jokes. I don't remember my parents punishing me, but I felt betrayed by my grandmother. I also felt embarrassed for saying something wrong.

What my 9-year-old self thought would be funny turned into a moment of shame. As part of this process, I worked hard on not blaming my grandma for what happened and instead kept asking myself, "How did I interpret myself from this unpleasant memory?" It was my first memory of feeling like I should be punished for what I said. Previous to this, I'd always felt a safety with my grandparents. They weren't here to discipline me; they were here to just love on me. But that unspoken code of safety was broken. I wasn't fully safe to be me anywhere or with anyone. There was always someone judging my behavior and sharing their disapproval with me.

I wrote down the words *betrayal, unsafe to say what I want, disapproval,* and *punishment for what I said.* Those were the words from which I began constructing the not-love self-beliefs that I'd unknowingly written and stored in my human operating system (my subconscious mind). Chapter by chapter, I opened my memories and pulled out conversations and moments that I remembered. The junior high trauma with my friend's mom had installed a long and diverse list of unhealthy self-beliefs. The beliefs that *I should be punished for what I say, I always say the wrong things,* and *it isn't safe to be me* were all fully integrated after that incident. So was the belief that I was fully *responsible for other people's feelings.*

I had no boundaries; I was a doormat for people to stand on and wipe their feelings and emotions all over, and I was powerless to stop them. So I accepted what they were feeling as my fault, and carried on trying to make them and anyone else who was mad at me love me. There was no room for joy anymore, because I was overburdened with everyone else's unhappiness.

I spent over a decade figuring myself out by returning to what I'd unknowingly taught myself from my own self-perceptions. I learned about the subconscious mind and how those secret programs were the beliefs that were really running my life. Those same beliefs also prevented me from fully loving myself. I had no idea what I wanted, even when it came to making plans for the weekend, because I was so filled with self-distrust that I waited for someone else to choose.

Along the way, I had attracted several friends who came unglued at me for something I'd said or done. In fact, at some point I didn't believe I deserved friends. In junior high my friend's mom had told me that, and so had my husband during a fight. Both events created a powerful and not-loving suggestion that I adopted as my subconscious self-belief. There was no way I could love myself when my subconscious suitcase was packed with beliefs that were the opposite of love.

In my younger days, people would have pegged me as outgoing, but as I felt less and less confident in who I was and what I had to say, I became more withdrawn. I hated large gatherings where I had to initiate conversation with strangers. It wasn't safe to put myself out there. Conflict sucked me under and buried me like quicksand. I understand these feelings now. As a person who took responsibility for everyone's feelings including my own, conflict directed at me became too much for me to shoulder, thus I sunk deeper and deeper into an unhappiness that most people didn't even know was there.

The self-beliefs from my childhood, the ones that told me I was loveable and important, kept me afloat until I had the trust and self-confidence to stand on my own two feet. They gave me the courage to start understanding myself so I could become self-aware and return to the self-love that communicated to me that I did matter and that I was a valuable person who was entitled to feel happiness and live a joy-filled life. They buoyed me until I believed that what I wanted, what I thought, and what I said were important, and that people would be interested in what I had to say.

They gave me the inner knowing that I deserved all of the abundance, laughter, and success that my mind could imagine. When I make a mistake, I'm not an embarrassment, I am just being human and learning through my missteps and my wins.

I felt deep compassion for all of the wounds my inner child's self-perceptions unknowingly brought into my adult life, and an empathy for how those self-beliefs contributed to the unhappiness I had created for myself as an adult. Conversely, I also felt an unlimited supply of gratitude for all of the self-beliefs that fed my self-love spark, and appreciation for all of the goodness that happened, even within the folds of my fears and self-distrust.

Despite all of the reasons that I didn't love myself, life was still a magnificent collage of children, an amazing business, incredible family support, travel, and good times with a few very good friends. The beauty of the good times and not-so-good times (duality again) filled my eyes with tears of happiness. I realized the only person I could change was me. Every minute of the last 15 years of understanding my story so I could understand myself has rewarded me with the freedom to be my authentic, quirky, passionate self. My story has been my greatest gift, because it made me who I am, past and present.

What is your story? Your story is important because it has made you who you are. If there are parts of your story (past) that aren't serving your love of self, have the courage to lean in and start unraveling the threads of self-beliefs that are holding you back from living a life which says, "Yes! I can, I am safe to be me, and I am free to create what my heart most desires." Your self-love translates to happiness and joy, which is infectious to everyone who is around you.

Along the way to understanding my story, after meeting the woman who worked with the subconscious mind, I learned from her how our self-beliefs, the ones we unknowingly accumulate and store in our sub or below awareness mind, create our life. We are conscious of how we feel and what is happening in our lives, but we are not conscious of why exactly we are feeling triggered, afraid, or unhappy— the beliefs that keep us from fully loving ourselves. For example, if I had been able to say what I wanted and needed to say, then I would not have felt fear and anxiety rise within me when I was confronted. I would not have experienced an emotional response that turned into a long-term feeling, because there wouldn't have been a subconscious self-belief igniting my need to feel afraid. In working with her, it confirmed what I knew all along, that my life's many stories (my past) contained the information that was creating my present feelings and my behaviors.

Once I'd discovered all of the unhealthy self-beliefs that I'd become from living my story, I took the steps to delete them from my human operating system, my subconscious mind. There are many ways that people work with the subconscious mind, but in all of my years of deep self-discovery, the technique that has worked the best and is the fastest for me is the modality created by the former hypnotherapist.

Understanding your story is a bridge to love's other 5 actions. It is the basis for deeply understanding your feelings and your behaviors. It connects you to your inner child's joys and to your suitcase of wounding, all the while building your self-compassion and empathy. Start with your story because it will lead you to the other side of the remaining *Love's 6 Actions.*

Discern Instead of Judge

Our human operating systems are programmed to judge. We judge ourselves. We judge others. We suffer others' self-beliefs when they judge us for how we look, what we say, and how we behave. Some believe that God supposedly judges us and determines whether we've been good enough to earn their (gender neutral) approval. If we aren't good enough for God because we don't always do the "right" things, then how can we be good enough for ourselves? We feel like we are always being judged. Our personal and collective relationship with judgment is an elusive and complicated conundrum for us to figure out. Not being good enough for others and for God makes it extraordinarily difficult for us to be enough for ourselves, and that makes fully loving ourselves a challenge.

Judgment arises from fear and lack's dark void. When other people judge us, it works like a suggestion to our subconscious mind. We, without discernment, adopt their judgment about who we believe ourselves to be. When my friend's mother judged me for saying something she didn't like, I accepted her judgment as my truth. Her anger and my belief that I was responsible for her feelings force fed me a smorgasbord of self-beliefs that I unknowingly adopted from her judgment. For example, my mind imprinted self-beliefs that told me, *I say things people don't like so that makes me worthy of punishment. I am bad. My words cause hurt and trigger people's anger.* That experience stuffed me with shame, embarrassment, self-punishment, victimhood, self-disappointment, and the belief that I didn't deserve to have friends. I unknowingly overindulged myself with not-love self-beliefs as a result of her judgment. When has this happened to you? Who were the people that from their judgment of you caused you to overindulge and create not-love self-beliefs?

My friend remembers as a young teenager that her uncles teased her for being too high maintenance for men. Teasing someone for something that could be hurtful is judgment hidden in supposed humor. It took her years to reverse the self-judgment she adopted from their judgment. When she was on a date, she held back from being her authentic self, because she didn't want to be too much. From other people's judgment, we morph into our most harmful critic. Their judgment ends with their comment, but the self-judgment we take from that moment stays with us until we become self-aware and realize that what they said was not the truth of who we are.

When others offer their judgments about you, those judgments filter through your self-perceptions, contaminating your human operating system with self-beliefs that move you away from self-love into the state of not loving yourself. Until you become self-aware and are able to discern that other people's opinions of you are "fake news," judgment's bitterness will sour your ability to be comfortable as your authentic self. Self-love that should roar like a bonfire gets turned down to a flicker as you process the fallout from judgment, that of others and also self-judgment.

Using discernment to process what others say about you can filter out judgment's poisonous sediment. It gives you the mental space to determine if what was said about you is your truth or not your truth. Discernment invigorates your self-awareness with the insight that the person pointing their judgmental finger at you is pointing three fingers back at themselves. Discernment helps you know that the other person's judgments originate from a place of not loving themselves. People that fully love themselves don't judge others. They understand, allow, forgive, accept, and respect others. People that fully love themselves are able to discern instead of turning those judgments into more self-judgment. Judgment without discernment adds up to too many not-love self-beliefs.

Discernment's muscles become atrophied from too many years of too little exercise. It is time to become self-aware and end the cycle of judging yourself based on how you believe others are judging you. If you believe for any reason that you aren't enough, take the time to stop judging yourself and discern *why* it is you think you aren't enough. "Why do I judge myself for not being good enough?" "Why do I judge myself for how I look?" "Why do I judge myself for being my authentic self, and conversely, why do I judge myself when I am not being my authentic self?" Discernment gives your self-love the elbowroom to grow, while judgment causes you to fit into someone else's perceptions and expectations.

The resulting self-judgment has swept us away in storms of not-love. Those storms have wiped out the infrastructure that our self-love should have been built upon. It is time to stop judging yourself for any reason and begin discerning the truth of who you truly are. Judgment causes hurt, but discernment causes wisdom. Judgment and discernment are part of duality's role in creating an experience for you. Are you ready to evolve beyond self-judgment so you can create an experience that nourishes your goodness instead of what has previously put not-love feelings and behaviors on repeat? Discernment changes your subconscious human operating system's code by putting self-love's empowerment back into your self-beliefs. Discernment as a part of *Love's 6 Actions* is a personal choice fueled by your self-awareness.

Allow Yourself to Grow Through Experience

Allowing permits you to grow in wisdom from your life's experiences. Your soul signed up for a set of experiences for you to learn from and grow beyond. When you can step back and look at your life through the lens of information instead of intense feelings of blame, guilt, shame, embarrassment, not-enoughness, rejection, or any other not-love feeling your experiences caused, it enables you to step aside and observe the experience for what it was, an experience filled with information about the self-beliefs you adopted. Allowing yourself to grow from your experiences takes all that you've suffered and reframes the sting of your suffering into a panoramic view of the self-perceptions that you, without self-awareness, created from your relationships and the ecosystem of your environment.

What experiences did you sign up for? What experiences caused you mental and emotional suffering? What information about yourself did you glean from that experience? What experiences are you here to evolve beyond? Try to find the patterns that you keep repeating. Those patterns contain loads of clues about what experiences your soul signed up for.

Allowing yourself the freedom to grow through your experiences enacts grace's compassion and generous spirit. When you accept the wisdom that your soul is here to grow through experiences, you give yourself the permission to discern what you've learned instead of judging yourself and others. Understanding, discerning, and allowing starts your self-evolution. Stop being so hard on yourself, and take the time to figure out what you are here to experience so you can create a life full of experiences that frees your soul to engage with more love, more joy, and more peace.

Within your journey back to self-love there are many experiences that have to be explored and analyzed through discernment so you can grow in self-understanding. Understanding my story and learning to discern instead judge, empowered me to uncover the hidden information that I'd unknowingly created about myself through my many life experiences. I am still traveling towards 100% self-love, but I am closer today to unconditionally living the all-things-good energy of love than ever before.

You are here to evolve back to self-love. Allow yourself the opportunity to grow into that love by learning about yourself from your life's experiences.

Forgive Because You *Understand*

Forgiveness is a process of letting go of blame. It doesn't mean you are condoning someone's actions, but that you've been able to seek an understanding so deep that it empowers you to release your emotional charge. Forgiveness is a letting go of the past that relieves you from the mental and emotional suffering of an unhappy experience. *Love's 6 Actions* empower forgiveness, because seeking understanding of your and others' experiences activates compassion for yourself and the person that hurt you. Forgiveness is a process of pardoning the person that hurt you and freeing yourself from your role in that relationship.

When you hang onto what needs forgiving, you are only hurting yourself. In my experience, forgiveness, like loving yourself and being able to offer love as an action, is a very nonlinear process. It would be great if you could one-by-one make your list and start forgiving those who hurt you. For me, I believed I'd completely forgiven someone, and then a memory would resurface making me realize that I still had more forgiving to do.

The processing of *Love Ignites Peace* taught me about myself and the human experience. As *Love's 6 Actions* took shape in my mind, I knew that forgiveness was made easier once I understood that I and every person that hurt me had a story which influenced who they became and how they acted. As I discerned the reasons (self-beliefs) behind their behaviors and mine, my compassion grew. And once I had the knowledge that our souls chose a set of experiences to evolve from, letting go of my past hurts became easier.

Forgiveness is less burdensome when you take the time to understand your own story and the story of the person who hurt you. It was their not-love self-beliefs installed from their life experiences that caused them to lash out at you. Using discernment helps you to move beyond judgment for yourself and for others as you understand the whys behind their behaviors. In order for us to create experiences, we have to be in relationship with each other, and we know that through duality's challenges that we haven't always chosen love's end of duality. None of us are exempt from this. We all play a variety of roles for each other.

In my marriage, my husband often played the role of intimidator and interrogator because that is how his operating system was programmed as a child. I played the role of disempowered victim, which was how my human operating system was programmed.

As we fought, his self-beliefs confirmed what he believed, and mine confirmed what I believed about myself. He incited conflict because it was what he knew, and I took responsibility for his feelings because it was what I knew. The information from our life's experiences played out as the pattern of our behaviors toward each other. We both wanted to be loved, but our self-beliefs triggered our deepest wounding.

The roles we played for each other brought all of those mental and emotional injuries to life. Our souls had chosen a set of experiences and we were the actors playing our roles for each other, until self-awareness caused me to take responsibility for my role in the behaviors we kept repeating over and over for each other. The only person in the relationship that I could change was me.

Forgiveness arose within me when I became tired of carrying his pain and mine too. My husband's soul signed up for a difficult set of experiences so that he could give his soul what it needed to evolve into his ability to love himself. Also, so he could give me the experience my soul desired; to be able to love myself as I stood confidently in my personal power. Forgiveness for him and for myself happened as I understood both of our stories, and I was able to discern instead of judge how we both came to believe about ourselves.

We've been taught math, reading, writing, and science, the intellectual basics, but we have not been taught how to process our emotions and how to take responsibility for what we are feeling. Our emotions contain encyclopedias full of information about ourselves. When we feel a strong emotion there is usually a subconscious self-belief that has triggered our emotional response. Learning how to mine your emotions is another way to uncover your secret self-beliefs. Emotional illiteracy has perpetuated the behaviors that project our insecurities, our bottled up anger, and our fears onto other people.

My big breakthrough in realizing that I believed I was responsible for everyone's feelings didn't come from my relationship with my husband, but with a friend. My daughter had recently joined me in working for *Love Ignites Peace*. I had no idea that my friend who owned her own business wanted the position. I triggered her when at a networking event I spoke about what my daughter and I were working on and didn't mention her. This incited her anger towards me and my daughter. Like my previous behavior patterns, I accepted her pain and took responsibility for her feelings. Like always, it was my fault. I had said something wrong. How could I make her see how sorry I was that I'd hurt her?

Months later we were still going back and forth, and she would not let go of what happened. Our relationship was suffering as was our joint project. Through the council of a wise friend, I finally had the realization that I believed I was responsible for not only her feelings, but everyone's feelings. The role that she played for me helped me to gain this huge leap in my self-awareness. I don't claim to know what role I played for her, but I do know that this experience contained big advances for us both in our self-growth, and it required forgiveness.

My friend's soul also signed up for a difficult set of experiences for her soul's growth. Through her experiences she gave me one of my most profound gifts of self-awareness. I couldn't love myself if I had no boundaries and was responsible for everyone's feelings. With this wisdom, I walked right into forgiveness's freeing expanse.

I had to forgive my grandmother for long ago telling my parents I was telling dirty jokes, and I had to forgive myself for believing I'd done something that made me an embarrassment. Mrs. Albertelli has been my most challenging relationship to forgive. I've struggled with letting go of a random adult rampaging my 12-year-old psyche for saying something she didn't like. Part of my challenge with letting this go is that I don't know Mrs. Albertelli's story or why she decided to come after a little girl without talking to her parents first. But, as I've investigated the patterns of my not-love self-beliefs and have gained an understanding of the human experience, I know that her actions set me up for creating the life which allowed me, through my experiences, to return to my power—love. Though I don't understand why my words triggered her so much, I recognize that her mental and emotional pain incited her behavior towards me.

It took me 44 years to fully forgive my friend's mom, and boy, does it feel great to not be carrying her pain (that became my pain) any more. I have also forgiven me, as a little girl, for unintentionally saying something that was hurtful to her. I've let go of the guilt and the shame, two very low frequency emotions that prevented me from loving myself and forgiving others.

My husband has been a powerful teacher on this journey to self-love, self-acceptance, and forgiveness. I've forgiven myself and him for all of the not-love words we said to each other over the years. I understand his story, and I've spent many years discerning the whys behind his behaviors and mine too. I've allowed myself the space and time to grow from that experience. I've forgiven my friend and other friends for how I've made them feel and how they've made me feel. I've forgiven myself for not having any boundaries with people and by being a relentless people pleaser.

We create our lives by playing a long list of roles for each other, so that we can give each other the set of experiences that our souls sign up for. Life isn't random happenstance; it is a well-choreographed dance of potential relationships all lined up to provide us with the experiences that our souls' desire. As I've reflected back on the many experiences which have hurt me, what I discovered were the not-love self-beliefs that I'd either acquired or expressed during that experience. This self-awareness caused me to realize that each painful interaction had gifted me with a huge opportunity to grow beyond my not-love self-beliefs. Forgiveness is so much easier when you discover the gift of self-growth/soul-growth that is hidden within every experience.

Forgiving yourself and others is an action that is well worth the effort. Forgiveness will free you from the wounding that others have projected onto you. Forgiveness will free you from the wounding you caused others because of your own hurt. Forgiveness frees you to let go of humiliation, despair, blame, shame, regret, guilt, anger, and fear— the noise of self-beliefs that keep you from loving yourself and enjoying life. Forgiveness allows you to grow from your experiences. You can't change the past, but you can change how you experienced it. Forgiveness promotes freedom.

Accept Yourself

Acceptance challenges you to love yourself exactly as you are, no matter where you are in the process. Self-acceptance paints a wide stroke, as you accept that you are imperfectly perfect as you negotiate your life's many experiences. As you battle the mental demons your not-love self-beliefs have created, acceptance teaches you to find the goodness within yourself regardless of what you believe.

As duality demonstrates, you are both the light and the dark. The shadows that dim your inner light and blot out your self-love are a part of you, just like the inner fire that supports your love of self. Because you are innately love, that means you are also innately good. Self-acceptance helps you understand the role duality has played in creating your life, while without judgment or pressure, it gently encourages you let go of what is causing your mental and emotional suffering so you can evolve towards your light. Self-acceptance helps you discern that you are navigating your life's many experiences. Spend less time judging your missteps and more time learning from them.

Your soul signed up for unique experiences, thus, no one on the earth is exactly like you. Accept who you are, even if others have made you feel unaccepted. The more that you stand authentically in who you are, the more empowered you become. There is no right or wrong (balanced duality) in how you express, just be who you are.

My teeth and gums suffered because a virus had taken up residence in my mouth's hard pallet. That virus was being fed with gluten, which is why when I eliminated gluten from my diet my gums stopped bleeding. But the virus was still there and its damage continued to wreak havoc on my dental health. I was told that I would lose my teeth. I did my best to not buy into this belief. I fought hard and tried a dozen different modalities to heal what had been injured. The thought of losing some of my teeth kept me up at night. My mind spiraled. Finally, one morning when I was meditating it occurred to me to ask why I couldn't accept myself, even if I lost some of my teeth.

I asked my subconscious mind to bring the answers to my conscious mind. Within the silence, I listened without judgment. My heart opened with compassion and my mind relaxed. The answers started arriving in the form of questions. "Who would love me if I didn't have my original teeth?" "Would people think I lost my teeth because I wasn't smart enough to take care of them?" "Would I be less attractive, thus less desirable?" The questions turned into statements. "I wasn't enough to love without my teeth." "No man would ever love me if I didn't have my original teeth." "I would be judged." "People would think less of me."

My inability to accept myself without having all of my teeth was rooted in a list of not-love self-beliefs that I knew I had to overcome so I could accept myself and whatever happened. This situation pushed me to surrender, and within the surrender my answers arrived. I cleared those beliefs from my subconscious mind, let go of my suffering, and accepted (loved) myself with or without all of my teeth. This experience allowed me to shed another layer that was causing me to mentally and emotionally suffer which was preventing me from accepting and loving myself.

Ask yourself what is causing you to not fully (unconditionally) accept yourself. You must accept yourself before you can fully love yourself.

Learning self-acceptance helps you know you are loveable just the way you are, even if you don't believe you meet the physical or intellectual standards that culture, the media, or others have installed into your beliefs. Self-acceptance helps you acknowledge the messiness of your life and says you are perfect and lovable in spite of it all. Self-acceptance frees you from suffering.

Respect Yourself and Your Unique Journey

Respect is another word for love. This thought came to me in a dream. That morning, the sunrise shed light on this 2am insight as I sipped my morning tea. Life and all of its experiences, like love, are unceasing. Life continues and within it love continues, regardless of how the not-love side of duality has tried to stop it. You are love in action regardless of what you believe about yourself, because respect conveys that no matter who you are or what you've experienced, you matter. As part of life's unceasing expression you are a valuable expression of life who is here trying to master love.

Criticism, blame, and shame are the opposite of respect. Offering myself respect meant letting go of the not-love self-beliefs that kept me feeling like I was those limited and unhealthy things. Once they were released I could, now with self-awareness, begin projecting *Love's 6 Actions* into all of my relationships, especially the one with myself, instead of my not-love self-beliefs.

Learning to respect myself was another piece of my journey to loving myself. It took me many years to advocate for my mental and emotional needs. When I was living without strong boundaries, I allowed other people to make their not-love baggage part of my own. Once I finally realized I was assuming responsibility for everyone's feelings, I knew I was giving my power away, and that this (giving my power away) was disrespectful to who I was: a significant, valuable individual.

It was easy for me to blame someone else for how I was feeling and easy for others to blame me for how they were feeling. Respect creates boundaries and a self awareness through wisdom that says, "The only one responsible for my feelings is me. If I don't like how someone is treating me, then I need to communicate my needs or change the relationship.

Understanding respect helped me to know that I was the supreme authority, the sovereign of my own life, and as such the only person I was responsible for is me. Just like everyone else was having their own unique experiences, so was I. That made me responsible for my own feelings, and made the people in my life responsible for their own feelings.

Respecting my unique journey didn't preclude me from acting with *Love's 6 Actions,* it encouraged me to offer *Love's 6 Actions* to myself and others. The fruit of empathy and compassion grew sweet within my ability to let go of control and allow other people to have their own experiences without me assuming responsibility. Respect taught me that helping others is different than mentally and emotionally trying to rescue them. Every time I took responsibility for another person's experience, I was potentially robbing them of what they needed to learn about themselves from their life experience. Respect was the last ingredient that allowed me to embody my authentic self and claim my full power as a unique individual who is one with her human community.

Respect aids me in offering honor and appreciation for myself, and for you, as a human beings negotiating life's experiences within duality's challenges. Respect helps me to honor what I've been through, and it pats me on the back for my resilience.

When you make a choice to live *Love's 6 Actions - Self Love*, you are also choosing to live *Love's 6 Actions - Love of Others*. Our lives are connected through our relationships; it is how we learn about ourselves and how we learn about each other. Relationships are how we create our experiences. Now that you have read this chapter, know that there is wisdom which crosses over into offering *Love's 6 Actions - Love of Others*. Though *Love Ignites Peace* is a parallel journey of loving yourself and loving others, those parallel paths cross and then split, over and over until you've mastered living love as an action. The mastery comes when those parallel paths finally merge into one path that connects your heart and your mind with the hearts of our collective human community.

ASSIMILATING CHAPTER 7:

Identify your own experiences within each of Love's 6 Actions – Love of Self

Understand Your Story

_____

_____

_____

_____

_____

_____

_____

_____

_____

_____

_____

_____

_____

_____

_____

_____

_____

_____

Our Next Evolution

_____

_____

_____

_____

_____

_____

_____

_____

_____

_____

_____

_____

_____

_____

_____

_____

_____

_____

_____

_____

_____

_____

_____

_____

Discern Instead of Judge

_____

_____

_____

_____

_____

_____

_____

_____

_____

_____

_____

_____

_____

_____

_____

_____

_____

_____

_____

_____

_____

Allow Yourself to Grow Through Experience

Forgive Because You Understand

_____

_____

_____

_____

_____

_____

_____

_____

_____

_____

_____

_____

_____

_____

_____

_____

_____

_____

_____

Accept Yourself

_____

_____

_____

_____

_____

_____

_____

_____

_____

_____

_____

_____

_____

_____

_____

_____

_____

_____

_____

Respect Yourself and Your Unique Journey

_____

_____

_____

_____

_____

_____

_____

_____

_____

_____

_____

_____

_____

_____

_____

_____

_____

_____

_____

_____

8

Love's 6 Actions—Love of Others

CHALLENGE: *Identify how you are treating others within each of Love's 6 Actions – Love of Others.*

Love's 6 Actions—Love of Others is your external code of conduct powered by your internal choice to master love. *Love's 6 Actions—Love of Others* also has two clear avenues, just like *Love Ignites Peace's* parallel pathways.

First, remember your words and actions directly influence how someone believes about themselves. Second, you have a choice to make, sandwiched within duality's love and not-love, in how you respond to other people's behaviors.

Love's 6 Actions—Love of Others has the power to *Ignite Peace.*

Understand Every Person Has a Story

As a collective human community, we are all connected through our stories. Though we've all created different experiences, we share the same emotions and feelings evoked by our life's stories. An infinite number of experiences can be explored, but our feelings and emotions express as a limited number of combinations. We know happiness's boundless enthusiasm and sadness's gloom. We are familiar with resentment's bitterness and hope's fresh flavors. Who hasn't felt awkward and out of place at some time? Or embarrassed? Or been made fun of? Or so filled with joy that they can't stop smiling? We share curiosity, wonder, confusion, anger, grief, boredom, excitement, heartbreak, envy, frustration, fear, vulnerability, enjoyment, and love.

Duality, like a devil on our shoulder, has whispered in our collective ears the reasons that have kept us divided. We look different from each other. We sit in different churches, mosques, or synagogues. We wear different clothes. We come from different countries and speak different languages. We belong to different political parties. A multitude of differences have separated us from each other, but why?

We are all here to create different experiences to learn and grow from. When we have that realization, we understand our differences are really what we have in common. We are all doing the same thing by learning from our unique set of experiences, no matter what those experiences are. Our emotions and feelings bind those unique experiences into unifying, relatable experiences for all of us. Our shared emotions connect us heart to heart through empathy's understanding.

When we take the time to understand someone's story, before allowing the duality of right and wrong to polarize our response, we diffuse actions that arise from misunderstanding and offer compassion instead. How we choose to respond empowers us to create a different experience for that person and for our collective human community. That person's story was the experience that caused them to become the person they are. What have they suffered? Their experience will be different from yours, but the feelings they've experienced from their story will be feelings you've probably experienced.

Maybe you were never verbally or physically abused, but because you've had other painful experiences in your life you can, through empathy, feel the hate or the rejection that person felt. We've all brought into our lives the self-beliefs we unknowingly adopted from our experiences. None of our parents were perfect; some were worse than others. A few in our collective human community have never known a mother and father's love. Maybe they had to worry where their next meal was going to come from, or they were in constant fear for their safety.

My friend was raped at 7 years old and then again at 15. Sexual, emotional, and physical abuse, or neglect of a child can hide behind a mansion's grand entrance, a multi-bolted door in an impoverished area, or a middle-class entryway in suburbia.

Understanding that every person has a story, which has influenced the self-beliefs that determine their behavior, strengthens your ability to offer understanding and compassion to the people that challenge you the most. It also boosts the knowledge that how you treat a person directly affects how they believe about themselves. It challenges you to overcome your own hurts and to not cause any more pain for others.

When you choose to walk the parallel path of *Love Ignites Peace*, understanding a person's story is a solid starting point. Taking the time to stand in that person's shoes, if only for a few minutes, activates your empathy. Responding to a person with this level of understanding doesn't mean you have to like them or that you condone their actions, it means you are choosing to create a different outcome by responding with *Love's 6 Actions*. Maybe that person just needs a hug instead of harsh words, or a smile instead of a scowl.

When we start responding with understanding, we begin living from love's end of duality's spectrum. Understanding a person's story opens our hearts to the unifying experience of our emotions and our feelings. It initiates an individual shift that, one person at a time, will spread to our collective human community. *Understanding initiates peace.*

Discern Instead of Judge

Discerning why a person behaves the way they do disarms the hurtful words and actions that can come from judgment.

Judgment is our go-to response. From God's supposed mighty wrath to viewing ourselves and each other as sinners (bad), our subconscious human operating systems have been programmed to operate from judgment instead of discernment. Our not-love self-beliefs are cut out of judgment's old and gnarled patterns. Our reasons for judging others are many. We judge others in order to make ourselves feel better about ourselves. Judgment relieves us of the responsibility for our own feelings. Judgment incites blame. Most of the time judgment bubbles up from a place of lack within us. Then there are the times that someone's actions hurt another person, either mentally or physically, and we judge them for those harmful actions.

I carried the belief I was not enough, therefore I judged others for their not-enoughness. When you feel frustrated, annoyed, or disappointed with someone, take a look in the mirror and ask yourself how those same qualities could be reflecting back to you.

As I explored my own judgments, I learned that what I judged someone else for was a belief about myself buried deep in my subconscious mind. When other people's actions frustrated me, I was reflecting a belief that said *I am a frustration*. People could only annoy me if somewhere deep inside I believed *I am annoying*. The same with disappointment and other qualities that promote not-love judgments.

A colleague used to call people he didn't like "tools." This one I had to look up in the *Urban Dictionary,* and when I read the definition, I could see the hand that he was pointing had three fingers pointing back at him. A "tool," as defined by the *Urban Dictionary,* is a person who thinks he is cooler than he is. That person usually has low self-esteem.

As I discerned the words and actions of both people, the one dishing out the judgment and the one the judgment was aimed at, I could see the low self-esteem working both ways, with each of them behaving, without self-awareness, so others would see them as "cool." Instead of judging them, I felt compassion for them because of the reasons that they didn't love themselves. We judge others to protect ourselves from the hurt we have suffered. As I discerned their individual stories, I began to understand the whys of their behaviors. One suffered a verbally abusive childhood and the other could never do enough or be enough for his father.

Gaining the awareness that I had been assuming responsibility for everyone else's feelings didn't absolve me of the responsibility for my own feelings. When you feel like judging someone else, ask yourself why. Take responsibility for your feelings. The reverse of this is also true; when someone judges you and makes you feel angry, ask yourself why their words triggered your anger. When other people don't act kindly towards you, take the time to ask yourself why their behavior caused you to feel the way it did. There is a list of juicy self-beliefs just waiting to float into your self-awareness. Use discernment to become more self-aware.

Discernment is a process of asking *why* a person bothers you and/or why you feel the need to judge another person, for any reason. When you take the time to look at your own set of whys, discernment allows you to activate your self-awareness. Using discernment moves you past blame to identify the root of your self-beliefs that were triggered by that person's judgments. When I was body shamed, I felt ugly and not good enough. That person's words triggered my feelings because I didn't believe I was attractive. Those judgments stung and created mental and emotional pain within me, until I became aware that the reason it hurt so much was because I believed those things about myself. The wounds of judgment.

Discernment helped me examine my own set of self-beliefs from this incident, and it helped me understand the story and discern the whys of the person that hurt me. Discernment allowed me to heal and transcend painful beliefs by getting to the root of my own suffering, then it helped me to forgive the person who hurt me. Letting go of judgment doesn't mean you have to like someone's behaviors. Their choices may not be what you'd decide for yourself, but you can choose to act with love and offer discernment instead of judgment.

People hurt and kill others every day. If they are caught, they are punished for their crimes. What if, during the process of finding them guilty or not-guilty, we took the time to discern why they behaved the way they did? Do people kill because they are bad, or did something from their life's story happen to them like neglect, or poverty, or abuse, or feeling unaccepted? From their stories, what happened to them seeded the subconscious self-beliefs that made them take actions to be accepted, seen, or heard. Negative actions are usually a cry for love's attention, but we have not been conditioned to respond with love.

My mom told me many years ago that the hardest people to love are the ones that need love the most. Discernment is the act of loving those who are a challenge to love, for many different reasons. Negative behaviors that shout out for love don't have to be as drastic as killing someone, they can take many forms. Take the time to understand that person's story so you can offer them discernment.

Discernment allows you to understand and have compassion for what they've experienced. It also helps you know that as a human being they matter, that they are important, and it helps you to care about them. When you remember that acting with love towards someone has the power to change how they believe about themselves, offering discernment instead of judgment becomes one of the greatest acts of love you can offer any human being.

Changing our judgmental behavior into discernment is one of love's most powerful actions. Offering discernment has the power to change people's lives for the better. *Discernment empowers peace.*

Allow Others to Have Their Own Experience

If you know that life is a set of experiences that every person's soul chooses, then why would you feel the need to control that person's experience? It is a question easier asked than put into action. I especially know this as a parent. When my children got older, I was challenged to turn off my need to protect them and allow them to have their own experiences. I thought I knew best and I didn't want to see them hurt. Allowing them to have their own experience and learn through their own mistakes might have been the most challenging of *Love's 6 Actions – Love of Others* for me to master. If their soul has signed up for an experience and I keep coming to the rescue or changing the outcome for them, then they will have to keep having this same experience in different forms, until they learn what they came here to learn.

My kids weren't the only ones I attempted to rescue or save. There have been many times where I jumped in with money or advice to pull someone from the burning building of their experiences. Yes, of course if a building was literally burning or they were physically in harm's way, that is a different situation. There are people who are not capable of taking care of themselves due to mental illness or because they are neurodivergent. Those people require help to survive. I am speaking specifically about rescuing a person from a mental and emotional challenge that their soul signed up for.

Maybe you don't think your friend should take that job, but your friend thinks there is no other choice. There is possibly a lesson embedded in that experience that your friend needs for her soul to grow. Maybe you have a family member that is always broke, but never takes action to change their circumstance. Will they ever change if you keep coming to their rescue?

Allowing a person to have their experiences is not to say, "I told you so." It is a letting go of your expectations, which empowers them and empowers you. Allowing helps you to relinquish your need to control. We control because we are afraid. Use *Love's 6 Actions – Love of Self* to understand your story and discernment to figure out why you need to control.

My Grandma Ruth, the one who reported me to my parents for telling dirty jokes, was born into a family that struggled to put food on the table for many years. Life was hard and survival was tenuous at times. Even as a young adult, she and my grandfather struggled for the first 15 years of their marriage to feel financially stable. When life started to look extra challenging she would say, "Tie another knot and hang on a little tighter." She was a mentally strong and tenacious woman, who through sheer willpower, made it through the tough times. Her life's story unknowingly taught her to be very controlling. She controlled from her own fears. If she didn't get her way, would she and her family be safe? Even when they were safe she controlled, because the lack of security she experienced in her life was in her subconscious human operating system, influencing her behaviors.

Grandma Ruth struggled with allowing others to have their own experience, especially my mom, her daughter, because of her subconscious programming. When you feel the need to control others, look to yourself first and ask, what am I afraid of? It could be that if you let go of control, you don't think people will love you, or that you won't be valued. Fear wears many hats.

My husband was my greatest gift and one of my most important teachers. If my parents had intervened and not *allowed* me to marry him, then I would not have had the experience to grow into my unconditional love of self and love of others. We came together, because our subconscious self-beliefs magnetized us to each other. The chaos and conflict we experienced together, through duality's challenges, birthed my personal evolution. I will forever unconditionally love him and myself for what we experienced together.

We learn through what seem like mistakes. We've judged mistakes as bad, when they are actually opportunities for us to learn more about ourselves. "Mistakes" are one of the best ways we learn about ourselves and others. I wish there was a word for mistake that had a positive connotation. There is not one ounce of me that considers my marriage a mistake, even though it ended in divorce. Maybe the word is blessing. Offer others the ability to make their own mistakes/blessings through their experiences by letting go of your need to control and allowing them their own very important experience.

Allowing empowers you to step back and know that this person has signed up for their own set of unique experiences for their self-growth. *Allowing creates space for peace.*

Forgive Because You Understand

Love, not a specific set of beliefs, is the glue that unites everyone in our collective human experience. *Love Ignites Peace* is not associated with any religion, but this story kept coming to mind as I was writing this section. As Jesus was hanging from the cross, he famously said, "Forgive them for they know not what they do." He was offering those who hurt him and others forgiveness, because he understood the human experience. We are all responsible for our own actions and our soul's growth, but the ability to take responsibility lies in a person's self-awareness.

We are all at different places on our self-awareness road trip. If you are reading this book, then self-awareness is something you are exploring. Not everyone is as self-aware as you are. They don't understand the complexities of the human experience, empowered by their soul's choices, nor have they taken the time to discern the whys of their feelings and behaviors. They will get there when we allow them to find their way, in their own timing. In the meantime, we can offer them forgiveness because we understand.

If they have not experienced compassionate and loving actions in their life or felt loved, how can they offer those same behaviors to others? Most people don't realize that it is the self-beliefs they unknowingly adopted from their life's story that are subconsciously running their lives. They are deaf to duality's noise and blind to their soul's choices. They can't change what they aren't aware of. They are seeking to be loved and valued, just like everyone else is, but they are doing it from a place that generates unloving and negative behaviors.

Forgiveness of others is a complex mental and emotional dance, which comes with a heavy, well over the 50-pound limit, suitcase of emotions that has to be examined from the wisdom of *Love's 6 Actions*. Forgiveness requires you to seek *understanding* of their story and yours. Forgiveness aids *dis-*

cernment of the whys behind behaviors and sees the big picture; that we are all here creating experiences for each other.

What if your souls actually agreed to have an experience that required forgiveness before you were born? Forgiveness *allows* everyone involved to learn more about themselves from their experiences. Forgiveness is a letting go of the expectation that the other person has the self-awareness to take responsibility for their actions, thus forgiveness *accepts* them as they are. Forgiveness *respects* that the person who hurt you is a human being, just like you. Forgiveness arises when your consciousness (self-awareness) evolves to a place where you desire to stop the cycle of pain and suffering, for yourself and others. *Forgiveness energizes peace.*

Accept Every Person as They Are

You can't make someone more self-aware with your judgment, you have to let go and accept them as they are. Just like you, every person is their own unique expression of duality. You have your qualities that you'd label as good, and then your qualities that challenge you. Life is not about being perfect all of the time, but about the journey back to unconditional self-love and love of others. As a collective human community, we are all on this very same self-discovery road trip; we take different routes, but our destination is the same. While on this lifelong trip, why not accept every person for who they are and how they've experienced their life?

What good has ever come from judging another person? What happens when we try to control another person's experience? Resentment is what happens, and a long list of other not-love feelings and behaviors. Acceptance gives us the wisdom to love a person right where they are as a participant in duality's challenging life experiences. Acceptance gives everyone a break and a chance to breathe.

Not-enoughness was a not-love self-belief that clung to me from every possible angle. From my intelligence, to my ability to be kind, to my physical appearance, I struggled to believe I was enough. Acceptance tells others, as you interact with them, that they are enough for you and for themselves, exactly as they are. Take a minute and imagine a world where we all believe we are enough for ourselves and each other. What does that feel like to you? Acceptance empowers people to show up in the world as their authentic selves. We all want to feel accepted for who we are, exactly as we are. Why not offer that acceptance to everyone you meet? *Acceptance makes peace possible.*

Respect Every Person

Every human being is equal in Love's eyes. Yes, I am intentionally personifying love. No one is better or worse than anyone else. We are all here having a unique set of experiences that connect us all through our relationships with each other. My soul's experiences were enabled by all of the people I've been in relationship with, and their soul's experiences have been influenced by being in relationship with me. Love is an energy that is at the center of every human being. Thus love, even when it does not feel like it, is at the core of every relationship. Our souls learn from being in relationship with each other.

How can I love someone who was mean to me or disrespected me? How can I love a parent who neglected me or even abused me? These are very personal questions about difficult life experiences. Love may not be able to be offered as a feeling, but love as respect for the experiences that you shared can be offered. When relationships challenge you, always ask yourself, "What am I supposed to learn about myself from this experience?" We are all on a journey back to loving ourselves. What did that experience teach you about yourself? Maybe that you are enough, lovable, and perfect, just the way you are regardless of what the other person told you or how they treated you. It requires an evolved level of self-awareness to be able to hear and to understand this message.

As we offer *Love's 6 Actions*, we know that there are people who have suffered unimaginable behaviors. These experiences are incredibly hard to understand. There are some people whose love spark has been so dimmed that it feels like evil is their pilot light. These people, though they exist and often get extraordinary attention for their not-love actions, are a very small percentage of our human community. And they too have a story filled with a set of awful experiences that extinguished their innate love.

For those who have suffered these people's actions, I send you so much compassion and respect for the unbeliev-

181

ably difficult experiences that you've been through. There are some actions that seem unexplainable, but I know for the majority there is purpose behind what we've experienced. Every experience in your life, no matter how awful and tragic, presents an opportunity for growth, evolution, and empowerment.

Respect is the sum of *Love's 6 Actions*. When you understand, discern, allow, forgive, and accept another person (and yourself) you are offering them the respect they deserve as a human being, negotiating this extremely challenging game of life. Respect is the root that nourishes the golden rule; treat others as you would like to be treated. You want others to regard your feelings, rights, and beliefs with respect. Offer that same consideration to others. No one is asking you to agree, just to be considerate, and to respect others' freedom to live their own choices by creating their own experiences. Respecting all choices creates harmony. *Respect is love in action which ignites peace.*

How *Love's 6 Actions*—Love of Others
Paves the Way for Peace

Understanding initiates peace.

Discernment empowers peace.

Allowing creates space for peace.

Forgiveness energizes peace.

Acceptance makes peace possible.

Respect is love in action which ignites peace.

ASSIMILATING CHAPTER 8:

*Identify your own experiences within each of
Love's 6 Actions—Love of Others*

Understand Every Person Has a Story

_____

_____

_____

_____

_____

_____

_____

_____

_____

_____

_____

_____

_____

_____

_____

_____

Discern Instead of Judge

_____

_____

_____

_____

_____

_____

_____

_____

_____

_____

_____

_____

_____

_____

_____

_____

_____

_____

Allow Others to Have Their Own Experience

_____

_____

_____

_____

_____

_____

_____

_____

_____

_____

_____

_____

_____

_____

_____

_____

_____

_____

Forgive Because You Understand

_____

_____

_____

_____

_____

_____

_____

_____

_____

_____

_____

_____

_____

_____

_____

_____

_____

_____

_____

Accept Every Person as They Are

_____

_____

_____

_____

_____

_____

_____

_____

_____

_____

_____

_____

_____

_____

_____

_____

_____

_____

_____

Respect Every Person

_____

_____

_____

_____

_____

_____

_____

_____

_____

_____

_____

_____

_____

_____

_____

_____

_____

_____

_____

_____

9
If Life and Mastering Love Were a Game

CHALLENGE: *Make two columns; label one*
column empowered and the other disempowered.
In what areas of your life do you feel empowered?
In what areas of your life do you feel disempowered?
What self-love in action steps can you take
to transform the disempowered to empowered?
Consider booking a Sub-Conscious
Transformation Session.

As I walked the parallel paths to learning about love through my own experiences, those paths often diverged and veered me into the oncoming traffic of the human experience. Those digressions hit me with life-changing wisdom. Based on what we currently know, our human consciousness (self-awareness) differentiates us from all other life on this planet. Through our mind's incredible abilities, we create our reality. Our mind thinks, it perceives, it interprets, it chooses, and from those different ways of thinking, it creates our beliefs. You are who you are because of your mind.

People have told you (made suggestions) what to believe about yourself, but it was your mind that adopted and adapted their suggestions to your self-beliefs. They created an experience for you, and your mind interpreted who you believed you were from that experience. Our powerful minds enable us with the ability to create our personalities and personal realities. In turn, our minds also have the ability to evaluate what we have created. I don't know of another species that has the ability to self-create and then to self-assess. If we want something different, we have the mental power to make a different choice.

If life and mastering love were a game, there would only be two rules (parallel tracks again of self-love and love of others).

First, *your mind is the master of how you experience your life. You are the beginning and the end, the Alpha and the Omega, of what you create.* The buck starts with you when your soul chooses a certain set of experiences, and it ends with you based on what your mind creates.

Second, *your words and actions directly impact the experiences that other people create for themselves.* We are all in relationship with each other. Those relationships create our experiences, and conversely, we influence other people's experiences. We are tethered through our individual and collective stories. What kind of influence do you want to be for others as they create their life?

Somewhere along the way we got sucked into a set of

beliefs that told us we were powerless instead of powerful. *Love Ignites Peace* is your personal self-awareness map back to empowerment. The ability to create the life and the world you desire starts in your mind. You have to believe that you are empowered enough to create a different reality; that you are the creator of your life, and then create the actions that empower those beliefs.

Through your beliefs, your mind is already creating your life and contributing to humanity's collective experience. Why not self-assess and choose beliefs that create an outcome that best serves you and our human community? This is part of walking the parallel path of love. Remember the fulcrum scale from the introduction? If enough of us believe that peace is possible, then actions will be taken and changes made that align with that belief. Peace will happen because your individual belief has joined with others who believe peace is possible, tipping the scales. It is up to you to start creating what you want in your heart and mind. If you feel a calling and a willingness to make the words *Love Ignites Peace* the lifestyle you want to live, then choose it, believe it can happen, and act accordingly. You will set the wheels in motion to architect a new consciousness.

Sovereign is a big and strange word that is mostly used to refer to royalty, but it is also relevant to you and your life. This is something we've forgotten about ourselves, because our subconscious human operating systems have been programmed with beliefs that tell us we need saviors and people smarter, richer, and more well connected to tell us what to do. This insight ironically paralleled my greatest fear; I wasn't smart or capable enough to take care of myself. That belief caused me to make 50 years of disempowering decisions.

You are already your own sovereign, the supreme authority, in this game of mastering love, because your mind at all times is creating your reality. This may feel scary, but it is also very empowering. Self-assess and ask yourself, where am I giving my power away to others? Are you looking for someone to rescue or save you? Where do you defer to others, because you don't trust yourself? Do you ever allow other people to make decisions, even when you know their decisions conflict with your moral compass?

When you decide unequivocally that you are going to be the sovereign of your life (even though you already are), that doesn't mean you misuse your power and try to dominate someone else; it means you, as the ruler of your life, have the power to choose, to become, and to create your life. If you choose to believe that love and peace can reign in your life and on the planet, you have the supreme authority to make that choice and then to make it happen.

Years ago I made a choice to stop watching the news. It wasn't that I was putting my head in the sand, it was just that I decided I no longer was going to buy into the reality that they were showing me 24 hours a day. The media was telling me what to believe. I decided to use my discernment and create beliefs that aligned with what I knew was possible for our human community. I knew this was possible, because while I was looking outside of myself to my human community, I was working on my inner life, my love of self, and transforming my own life to peace and joy.

My focus, first and foremost, was to transform my own mind, the self-awareness that was creating my consciousness. With laser intensity I started cleaning out my closet of beliefs that kept me from loving myself. Many of those beliefs were very personal to my life's story, but many of them were beliefs that culture and the media told me to think. We don't have to believe everything they show us and tell us. We have a choice to use our discernment.

Have you heard the statement that energy goes where attention flows? This is another reason I stopped watching the news. I didn't want to give my energy to the not-love and not-peace that the media was constantly showing me. My power lives within me and what I believe. That inner power is so great it creates my external reality. With all of my heart and all of my mind, I believe *Love Ignites Peace* is how our future can look. Believe it with me, and together our combined energies will put our attention towards the goodness in humanity, and our potential to create a loving, joyful, peaceful planet for all.

We have to believe we can create change,
then align our behaviors with the
change we choose to become.

I am not saying that tragically bad things aren't still happening, but I am choosing to believe that every human's true nature is goodness. When a problem person shows up, I try and understand their story because I know it is their self-beliefs, accumulated from difficult and not-loving relationships, which has put them on a destructive trajectory. If they believe they are no good, most likely that is because someone told them many times that they weren't any good. Being no good is what they believed they were, so that is what/who they became.

If we believe that people will always be fighting for resources instead of sharing, then fighting will continue. The power of suggestion is so strong that suggestions, good or bad, true or not true, can become our reality. We know that when we change our minds we change our reality.

So much of my life, I felt like life played me. I felt and acted powerless, letting situations and other people control me; I lived to please others, because I held so many not-love self-beliefs. I had to become aware that I am the master of my inner power and the creator of my own personal life's experience. Then I had to deal with all of my self-beliefs, my subconscious programming, which held me trapped in my self-created web of powerlessness. Finally, duality's tricky challenges woke me up to what I needed to choose in order to create love for myself, and treat others with that same love.

Gaining these awarenesses led me to mastering the right use of my energy—Love. Letting go of blame and victimhood wasn't easy, and for me it took revisiting *Love's 6 Actions* again and again until I could stop making others responsible for my experiences. Whether you like a challenge or not, you are already being challenged by life's game of returning to love. Do you want the game to play you, or are you ready to master the game?

If Life and Mastering Love Were a Game (The Cliffs Notes)

The Rules

1) The power of your mind, the conscious and the subconscious, makes you the sovereign creator of how you experience life.
2) Your behaviors influence how others perceive themselves.

This is all done in relationship with each other.

The Challenges/Obstacles to Overcome

1) The experiences that your soul chooses.
2) The complexities of your subconscious mind and its hidden self-beliefs.
3) Duality's influence on your experiences.

The Objective

To self-assess and become self-aware so you can master self-love and love of others.

ASSIMILATING CHAPTER 9:

*Make two columns. Label one column
Empowered and the other Disempowered.
In what areas of your life do you feel empowered?
In what areas of your life do you feel disempowered?
What self-love in action steps can you take to
transform the disempowered to empowered?*

Empowered   **Disempowered**

_____   _____

_____   _____

_____   _____

_____   _____

_____   _____

_____   _____

_____   _____

_____   _____

_____   _____

_____   _____

_____   _____

_____   _____

_____   _____

_____   _____

Empowered   **Disempowered**

_____   _____

_____   _____

_____   _____

_____   _____

_____   _____

_____   _____

_____   _____

_____   _____

_____   _____

_____   _____

_____   _____

_____   _____

_____   _____

_____   _____

_____   _____

_____   _____

_____   _____

_____   _____

10

The Love in *Evol*ve

Years ago, I remember writing the word *evolve,* and in a flash of insight, as I looked at what I'd written, the word *love* spelled backwards jumped out of my notebook and into my mind. I love a good wink from the universe, and this one left me giggling and talking out loud to myself. *Really, you've got to be kidding me! Is this another message that I and our collective human community need to pay attention to? Has the secret to humanity's evolution been hidden right before our very eyes?* The answer was emphatically, "Yes!" I don't believe it is an accident that the word love is found, not only spelled backwards in *evol*ve, but also scrambled, just in case we didn't catch it the first time (ev*olve*).

This message is stated pretty clearly: Love is the path of our next human evolution. It is what we need to become so that individually and collectively we can tip the fulcrum scales and evolve our human consciousness (self-awareness). *Love Ignites Peace* is an individual self-discovery road trip to our collective destination. It is the GPS that can guide us to our next evolution.

The words *Love Ignites Peace* dropped into my mind on a beautiful summer day, and now I am dropping them into your mind. Set your course and intend for the words *Love Ignites Peace* to guide you. Plant those words like seeds in your heart and in your mind. When you get off track *Love Ignites Peace* will reroute you back until you can walk the parallel paths of love as an action. *Love's 6 Actions* are rest stops for you to pause and reflect on all of your relationships, especially the one with yourself. There are no rules to follow, everyone's route is different, only your desire to choose the journey is required.

Take a minute right now, if you feel called, and set your intention for *Love Ignites Peace* to guide your personal evolution. It is up to you to put love's coordinates in your heart and mind. When your heart and mind unify and work in harmony, the love in evolve will blossom into your new consciousness (self-awareness).

Love Ignites Peace kindles that truth deep within us, and encourages us to evolve from the misuse of our power to the right use of our human consciousness—love in action. *Love Ignites Peace* reminds us to stop creating mental and emotional suffering, and to start loving ourselves each day so we can love without so many conditions.

When our human consciousness collaborates
with love, we become the master builders
of all things good.

Before I start building something new, I imagine what I want to create, and then I feel the end result. *What do you imagine a world living as Love Ignites Peace will look like*? I imagine a world where everyone has more than enough food, clean water, and resources for comfortable shelter. I imagine a world where we share our resources for the betterment of all. I imagine a world where everyone is safe. I imagine a world where we come together in collaboration and cooperation. I imagine a world where people live their passions and create from the whisperings of their soul.

I imagine a world where everyone feels free to authentically be themselves. I imagine a world where we create success for all. I imagine a world where people interact using *Love's 6 Actions*. I imagine a world that intentionally chooses the highest good for all life. I imagine our collective human community living in peace and harmony.

Building a society on love's foundation starts with you. You have a choice to make. You will always live on a dual planet, so you need to intentionally choose behaviors from love's end of duality. Your individual choices empower the *evol*ution of our collective human community.

> ***Love** is the path to healing your heart and your mind. You are the self-awareness that **Ignites** change. And **Peace** is the end result.*

Why love? Because love as an action is the evolution that can transform societies. Love creates all things good not just for some, but for all. When we choose *Love Ignites Peace*, we are igniting an individual choice that has the power to change our collective human experience.

I can't wait to hear about your travels and meet you at destination peace! Love is a high frequency energy. Once you master love, it opens a doorway to even higher frequency energies. Joy, freedom, abundance, and peace live on the other side of love's threshold. These are the qualities that, along with love, ignite the highest expression of your unlimited human potential.

Raise your frequency with Love Ignites Peace and step into your unlimited potential.

EXERCISE:
On the next page, write down any intentions this book has inspired for you. Set a specific intention for creating peace in all of your relationships, especially the one with yourself.

FOR FUN:
What does a world where everyone lives Love Ignites Peace look like to you? There is individual power in imagining such a place, which is magnified exponentially when we collectively imagine.

Join us by sharing you greatest imaginings for a world living as love in action at LoveIgnitesPeace.com/Our-Next-Evolution-Book or on Facebook at loveignitespeaceimagine.

Intentions

_____

_____

_____

_____

_____

_____

_____

_____

_____

_____

_____

_____

_____

_____

_____

_____

_____

_____

_____

_____

_____

Our Next Evolution

_____

_____

_____

_____

_____

_____

_____

_____

_____

_____

_____

_____

_____

_____

_____

_____

_____

_____

_____

_____

_____

_____

Appendix

Recommended Reading

You are the Placebo by Dr. Joe Dispenza

Becoming Supernatural, by Dr. Joe Dispenza

Man's Search for Meaning by Viktor Frankl

The Biology of Belief by Bruce Lipton, PhD

Dying To Be Me by Anita Moorjani

The Power of the Subconscious Mind by Joseph Murphy

The Journey of Souls by Michael Newton, PhD

Your Soul's Plan: Discovering the Real Meaning of the Life You Planned Before You Were Born, by Robert Schwartz

Love Money, Money Loves You by Sarah McCrum

Resources

There are many tools and talented people to help you evolve beyond the self-beliefs that have kept you from loving yourself and others. *Love Ignites Peace: Our Next Evolution, The Companion Journal* offers you a guided process to start your evolutionary journey back to love. It can be ordered at www. LoveIgnitesPeace.com/Our-Next-Evolution-Book.

You can listen to Paige and Ashlyn explore the *Love Ignites Peace* lifestyle on their podcast *Love Ignites Peace: Bathtub Chats*. The podcasts can be found on Apple, Spotify, Amazon, iHeartRadio, and our website at www.LoveIgnitesPeace.com/Our-Next-Evolution-Book.

The most effective tools that I have found to transform my self-beliefs are offered by our *Frēq MD'S* (we humorously call them frequency doctors). If you want to focus on your limiting subconscious programs, book a Subconscious Transformation session. If you need additional insight into your human experience, consider booking a Spiritual Energy Work session.

All of these tools to help you break through your glass ceiling of limitations and evolve into love are found at: www.LoveIgnitesPeace.com/Our-Next-Evolution-Book.

As always, I am cheering you on and sending you love from my heart to yours as you negotiate your many human experiences.

Acknowledgments

A gigantic thank you to AnnaBeth Davidson who has patiently and gently coached me over the last four years to become a better writer. This book would not exist without her insightful comments, keen editing abilities, and friendship. From the bottom of my heart, thank you AnnaBeth!

To my parents who created a foundation of self-love for me to build upon when I was ready, and for them allowing me, without judgment, to have the experiences I needed to grow. To Ian and Ashlyn, who have been with me since the day the universe delivered the message. Ashlyn has been unwavering in her love and my "we can do this" partner in bringing *Love Ignites Peace* to the world. She is my rock. I couldn't have done this without her. To Ian who, without hesitation, agreed to be one of my first readers, and for always having my back. To João for designing the most beautiful cover that I could ever imagine. To Tracy, Pen, Bill, and Emily and my entire community of supportive friends.

Thank you.

Endnotes

1) "Number 6 Meaning in Numerology," Accessed May 20, 2023. www.numerology.com/articles/about-numerology/single-digit-number-6-meaning.

2) Cherry, Kendra, "The Unconscious Mind, Preconscious Mind and Conscious Mind," February 23, 2023. scious-and-unconscious-mind-2795946

3) Lipton, Bruce (2005) *The Biology of Belief,* Hay House, 2015, Updated Editions, pg. 172

"Someday, after mastering the winds, the waves, the tides and gravity, we shall harness for God the energies of love; and then, for a second time in the history of the world, man will have discovered fire."
—Pierre Teilhard de Chardin

Connect with Paige

Thirty-three years ago, life transplanted Paige from her rural Iowa roots 5,280 feet closer to the bluest skies she'd ever seen. Now calling Castle Rock and Grand Lake, CO, home, she finds daily inspiration in nature's quiet peacefulness.

Paige's life took an unexpected turn in 2008, when out of thin air the words *Love Ignites Peace* landed in her conscious mind. This profound moment became a catalyst, shifting her path from successful business owner to student of love—the root of human potential. Mastering the deep meaning and embodying the wisdom in the statement Love Ignites Peace now guides her daily life. Paige's insights in *Love Ignites Peace: Our Next Evolution* invite you to return to the love that you truly are—awakening your highest potential and transforming the way you experience life. Paige is also the author of *Love Ignites Peace: Our Next Evolution, The Companion Journal*.

Invite Paige and her daughter Ashlyn for a workshop or speaking event that inspires deeper self-awareness and healthier relationships. Keep the conversation going by listening to their podcast Love Ignites Peace #BathtubChats. You can find more information at LoveIgnitesPeace.com/OurNext-Evolution-Book.

Love Ignites Peace